POLICE SU

POLICE SUICIDE

ACUITY OF INFLUENCE

Michael J. Alicea

DISSERTATION.COM

Boca Raton

Police Suicide: Acuity of Influence

Dissertation.com
Boca Raton, Florida
USA • 2015

ISBN-10: 1-61233-429-6
ISBN-13: 978-1-61233-429-5

Typeset by Medlar Publishing Solutions Pvt Ltd, India

Cover image by bsauter/Bigstock.com

ABSTRACT

According to the CDC (2005), suicide claims approximately 30,000 lives each year in the United States. The law enforcement profession is a dangerous profession that oftentimes dramatically influences an officer's perceptions of incidents often related to the repeated exposure to trauma. The intention of this research project was to explore the lived understanding of police officers regarding their acuity with respect to the subject of officer suicides. A qualitative phenomenological research was conducted, consisting of nine demographic and nine open-ended interview questions. Data were audio-recorded and transcribed throughout the interview process. The research project examined the awareness levels of police officers in a local metropolitan agency in Miami-Dade County, Florida. A review of the information provided by this research study resulted in five major themes focusing on (a) suicide prevention, (b) talking about suicide, (c) prevention training, (d) identifying available outside resources, and (e) understanding the police culture. The conclusions reached as a result of this research project could broaden the existing literature of suicide and may assist police administrators who may face the issue of police officers considering suicide.

TABLE OF CONTENTS

TABLE OF FIGURES

TABLE OF APPENDICES

DEDICATION

Good-bye, brother in blue all of us are thinking of you.

You left this world way too soon, for reasons only known to you.

If only one of us knew, we certainly would have reached out to you.

Good-bye, brother in blue. Rest in peace

(Johnson, 2010)

Officer Thomas G. McEvoy
Coral Gables Police Officer
09/27/52 – 10/22/99

"Rest in Peace"

ACKNOWLEDGEMENTS

I would like to thank my immediate family for their encouragement and continued patience with me throughout these last five years for which I was never available. At times I was quite the recluse and at times quite a difficult person to be with while in pursuit of this dissertation.

I would also like to thank the many police officers I have personally known who either died in the line of duty or fell victim to their own despair and abandonment. These officers dedicated their lives to saving lives, and it is a debt that will never, ever be repaid, because they paid with their lives. Lastly, to my friends and the fellow officers with whom I have worked these last 33 years; through their professionalism and resolve to always be their best, they enabled me to appreciate that each day we are alive is a gift.

I would also like thank the members of the Coral Gables Police Department who willingly and courageously spoke freely, truthfully and boldly about the issue of police suicide. I would also like to thank the members of the Miami Police Department for the valuable experience they provided me as a young and impressionable police officer during the tumultuous 80's.

Finally, I would like to thank my dissertation committee chair and adviser Dr. Samuel Pizzi for never losing faith in my ability to address and complete this valuable research study, and to Dr. Susan Ogeltree whose encouragement and support enabled me to never lose sight of the fact that I could complete this project. In addition, I would like to thank Dr. Dale Coovert, my advisor throughout these five years of study who always took the time from his busy schedule to talk to me and offer his professional support towards completing this dissertation.

CHAPTER ONE: THE PROBLEM

Problem Background

According to Kelly's (2005) research findings, the law enforcement profession is a hazardous occupation. In the aftermath of the 9/11 terrorist attack, Violanti, Castellano, O'Rourke and Paton's (2006) work also asserted that police officers who are often exposed to repeated distressing incidents over time may consider suicide as an option. Violanti's (2008) work on the issues of police suicide revealed that continual, demanding and distressing situations could eventually lead a police officer to be disposed to psychological issues. Police officers suffering from unresolved issues, as Kelly (2005) has asserted, in time risk their ability to make sound decisions and appropriate choices on the job, as well as in their private lives.

Research conducted by Kelly and Martin (2006) on the subject of whether suicide is real or not, in combination with Violanti's (2007) work on what he described as an epidemic in blue on police suicide, concluded that it was the foremost cause of death for police officers in the United States. When considering the subculture that is often characteristic of the law enforcement community, Burke and Mikkelsen (2007) have described the omnipresent nature of the profession. Kelly (2005) and Violanti et al. (2006) have described law enforcement as a profession that perpetuates an increased level of tension and distress which can lead to suicide as a real possibility. Tate's (2004) research revealed that the rate of suicide in the United States for police officer follows a trend that puts it at a higher frequency than the general population. Kelly and Martin, along with Violanti (2007) and Waters and Ussery (2007), suggest that the largely increased statistics on police suicides are related to the influences of alcohol, family conflicts, seclusion from one's fellow officers, hopelessness, and the accessibility of firearms. These trends and alarming statistics point out the need for a qualitative phenomenological study. It was hoped that this research model may help reveal and appreciate the lived experiences of police officers at a specific agency (The Coral Gables Police Department) in relation to the effect of a suicide that occurred there. This model may help comprehend the effect it had among other officers of the organization.

Significance of the Problem

According to Cross and Ashley (2004) and Waters and Ussery (2007), people who work in professions with increased levels of stress and trauma, as well as identifiable social role expectations, are often vulnerable to suicide ideation. Violanti and Samuels' (2007) research on the psychological perspectives associated with suicide, as well as Waters and Ussery, concluded that the law enforcement profession consistently makes vulnerable its employees and exposes them to a proliferation of stress-related heights of suffering. Waters and Ussery put forth the notion that the longstanding effects of stress often lead to an inability to cope effectively with daily situations.

According to the Officer Down Memorial Pages (ODMP, 2004 - 2010), a significant number of police officers (well within the 100+ range) die in the line of duty each year. Of noteworthy significance, within that length of time, police officer suicides averaged 400+ per year, contributing to what O'Hara (2009) concluded is a significant increase in law enforcement deaths nationwide. Waters and Ussery (2007) have also concluded that substance and alcohol abuse, as well as marital issues are major contributors of police officer suicide. Crank's (2004) research on police culture, as well as Lejoyeux et al.'s (2008) work on the characteristics associated with attempted suicide, asserted that it was often preceded by the use or abuse of alcohol when performed in union with a common police practice called "choir practice". Crank further asserts that the ritualistic performance of choir practice is usually associated with the excess consumption of alcohol by police officers in an effort to minimize the stress often associated with their work, and in the process facilitates an increased bonding with fellow officers.

Kelly and Martin's (2006) research on police suicides found that oftentimes, police officers who suffer from psychological disorders will often go to great lengths to disguise any signs of distress through the abuse of prescription and over-the-counter medications. By far, depression is the most common disorder related to suicide. Andrew et al. (2008) and Bertolote, Fleischmann, De Leo and Wasserman (2004) reviewed psychiatric diagnoses and the evidence associated with suicide; nationwide, those who are successful in committing suicide are often diagnosed with depression. While depression is a treatable disease, Andrew et al. and Cross and Ashley (2004) have indicated that it is an affliction that is often problematic at best to diagnose because it imitates the symptoms of other debilitating disorders, such as alcohol abuse, melancholy, exhaustion, and Post Traumatic Stress Disorder (PTSD). Accordingly, uncharacteristic symptoms of depression will very often mask the underlying disease. DePaulo Jr. and Horvitz (2002) indicate that a skilled therapist might misinterpret the hidden symptoms of depression and may make a misdiagnosis in the process. O'Hara (2009) and Violanti's (2009) research on suicide in general affirmed Tuck's (2009) findings with regard to integrating a spiritual element into law enforcement. They asserted that medicating oneself heightens the prospect of further disguising the symptoms of depression which frequently are ignored by a police officer's family and fellow officers.

According to Andrew et al. (2008), police officers who commit suicide, do so because they are often depressed. Waters and Ussery (2007) support the idea that an adequate peer support group system facilitates and can help overcome a police officer's inclination for isolation, in part due to learned helplessness caused by depression. Kelly (2005) concurs with Waters and Ussery that very often police administrators are uncertain as to how to effectively address problematic circumstances that can arise in their officers. Kelly, as well as Violanti (2003) and Hackett and Violanti (2003) concluded that the limited availability to psychological resources often leaves a police officer susceptible to depression and suicide. As is often the case, police officers are reluctant to seek the aid of police administrators and/or line supervisors and will oftentimes agonize alone. Crank (2004) suggests that there exists a concern with respect to trust and occupational segmentation between police officers and the administration. Police officers and police administration have distinct cultural norms; police administrators will insist on conformity of conduct through what is perceived as coercion. Crank goes on to say that cultural and operational differentiation will very often exist between the police officer and those in the administration and these disparities have a tendency to be noticeable over a period of time reinforcing a police officer's suspicion of the administration.

The administrative system is often difficult to deal with for many police officers, and is considered the leading cause of stress for many officers (Crank, 2004). Schafer's (2008) research concluded that administration and its managers represented a micro-managing quandary for most police offers. Schafer further asserts that micro-managing takes place when administrators do not permit police officers to develop as decision makers in their own right. He asserts clearly that police officers must be allowed to meet with failure from time to time. The ability to make mistakes in the field facilitates a police officers' professional growth, and can assert confidence in a police officer's judgment to make independent decisions. Schafer also states quite clearly that the inability of a police officer to exercise discretion in the way of decision-making practices can lead to stress and can cause officers to doubt their own competency levels.

In the process of demonstrating or masking the signs and symptoms of stress, Tuck's (2009) research revealed that there is a direct correlation to the declining mental health function of a police officer and the consequent vulnerability to any negative contact with the public. Kappeler, Sluder, and Alpert (1998) described this as the dark side of law enforcement. Kelly's (2005) research revealed that as a rule, police administrators are normally more concerned with out-of-place behavior and/or the misconduct of a police officer rather than with officers' health and ability to function at an optimum level. Waters and Ussery (2007) noted that although there are a wealth of preventative treatment programs available that focus on stress reduction, many police officers do not avail themselves of these programs.

In police departments, there is an overwhelming cultural negativity often associated with attending a mental health program and or seeing a trained mental health counselor. There is also an overriding correlation to what Kelly (2005) has described as deteriorating mental health functioning and relationship concerns at work and home. In addition, illnesses and mishaps on the job, and depression associated with self-medication compound the issue. The ability to function optimally in one's profession requires what Kelly has asserted is a well-balanced mental health attitude. Blum (2000) affirmed the concept that police officers live and work under pressure and are discouraged from seeking help. Accordingly, Diamond's (2003) research on the barriers to treatment and police officer suicide indicate that a police officer has no special immunity to depression.

Purpose of the Study

The purpose of this research project was to explore the lived experiences of police officers concerning their perceptions and or consequential effects with respect to police officer suicide. Neuman's (2005) social research methodology indicates that qualitative research facilitates the gathering of facts and evidence that would be recognizable in the form of signs, subjects and significance. The use of a phenomenological approach can facilitate detecting a police officer's ideation for considering suicide as a remedy when in turmoil and despair. Moustakas (1994) recognized the significance of being mindful of the role that perception plays in phenomenon research.

This research project examined the awareness levels of police officers from a local metropolitan agency in the Miami-Dade County, Florida. The Centers of Disease Control (CDC, 2005) classified police officers as being a high-risk population with a high propensity rate of suicide. Male police officers are more apt to commit suicide than their civilian population counterparts and twice as likely to commit suicide as their female counterparts (CDC). Because of this alarming statistic, further study is warranted.

Research Question

The following research question constituted the core of this dissertation project:

What are the lived experiences concerning the incidence of suicide among law enforcement officers?

Open-Ended Interview Questions

Data collection consisted of a series of interviews whereby police officers were queried on nine demographic items in addition to nine interview questions. It was hoped that having police officers involved in this research project may prove useful in providing awareness and acquaintance of their lived experiences. As such, this may in fact contribute to understanding the probable factors that mental health plays on police officers, and the level that stress plays when personal safety is an issue.

The interview questions were comprehensive, permitting the police officers to expand upon them when needed. The demographic questions were:

1. What is your gender?
2. What is your race?
3. What is your age?
4. Are you a sworn law enforcement officer with Coral Gables Police Department in the County of Miami-Dade, Florida?
5. What kind of law enforcement organization are you working with (State, County or Municipal Agency)?
6. What title (Police Officer Sergeant, Lieutenant, Major, Assistant Chief or Chief of Police) or position do you have with your law enforcement organization?
7. How many years have you been employed as a sworn law enforcement police officers?

The list of open-ended questions that were used in this research project included the following:

1. What type(s) of difficult situations have you or another police officer come across in your law enforcement career that would lead you to consider suicide as a choice?
2. In respect of your experience with your present law enforcement organization, what type of in-service educational program did you undertake concerning the topic of suicide?
   Thinking back on the training you received with your present agency, what could have been done to improve and enhance the efficacy of the suicide education (if any)?
3. Considering your experience with the agency with which you are employed with, what ways does your police organization demonstrate concern about your welfare including the issue of suicide?
4. What efforts do your peers make to diminish the strains that depression often exerts on fellow officers who may consider suicide as an option?
5. How do you view the police culture encumbering an officer from the ability to look for help on the subject of suicide?
6. In respect of your experiences with your present law enforcement organization, what types of training programs have you had that would have addressed the issue of suicidal thoughts?
7. How do police supervisors and command staff speak to the issue of police officer suicide in your law enforcement organization?
8. How can police supervisors and command staff ward off the risk of suicide as an option for your fellow officers?

Limitations and Delimitations

As Neuman (2005) has asserted, in-person interviews limit a police officer's ability to be honest, given the time constraints that are often a precipitating factor. Allowing for time constraints, police officers may have been inclined to hurry through an interview for the sake of completing the process. Very often, time was measured with respect to one's particular work issues; these were easily resolved accordingly by prearranging appointments at a time that is appropriate for the police officers. On the whole, individuals may be prejudiced, and these feelings and opinions may have a place in a qualitative research study. Qualitative investigators do not endeavor to oversimplify the results acquired; rather, complexity can afford a distinguishable degree of examination of the phenomenon (Moustakas, 1994). In the face of scant research on police officer suicide and the misclassification of police officer suicides, it was reasonable to assume that there was a significant limitation of truthfulness by police officers with regard to the questions offered.

Crank (2004) asserts that a participant's reluctance to being forthright when answering sensitive questions may be in part due to the subject matter. The somatic and sometimes emotional difficulties encountered can create limitations and may deter a police officer's ability to be open. In an effort at thwarting such limitations, the following steps were taken with all police officers in order to safeguard their participation in the interview process.

1. Police Officers were permitted sufficient time to answer all questions.
2. Police Officers were permitted sufficient time to have any of their requests answered.
3. A participant's questions or concerns were addressed when solicited.
4. In an event that a participant requested a break, adequate time was afforded for the request.

Moustakas (1994) indicates that qualitative research design allows for copious explanation of the phenomenon being researched, which provides reliability and credibility to the responses. Taking into consideration all the steps needed to facilitate openness, appreciating that a police officer's explanations can adjust with time was weighed.

In recognizing the generalizability of this type of research, Creswell (2005) asserts that the preparation and assessment of a qualitative research project requires an aptitude for drawing accurate interpretations from the data, and subsequently applying them to the research conditions. Creswell advances the concept that for external credibility, participants should be randomly selected.

In order to increase the transferability of the research, a random sample of participants was selected from the Coral Gables Police Department. Transferability was correlated to the results of the research and were applied to the population of the law enforcement community on a larger scale, i.e., within the County of

Miami-Dade (Neuman, 2005). According to Crank (2004), since law enforcement organizations are generally regulated by their various jurisdictions, they can have differences in training and educational requirements, as well as in the police culture itself. A smaller sample size limits the possibility of transferability to the greater population.

Definition of Terms

The following is a list of definitions which are a part of the familiar lexicon often associated with the law enforcement community. Terms and jargon that are emblematical to a particular profession, in particular law enforcement, very often have dissimilar meanings to the public in general.

Brotherhood denotes a sense of solidarity between the men and women of a police organization. It represents a form of honor and solidarity in the law enforcement organization, encouraging allegiance and constancy and *esprit-de-corps* (Cranks, 2004).

Choir Practice denotes a ceremonial time that police officer's drink with one another as a way of reveling together with no consideration to rank differences (Crank, 2004). Choir practice often happens during off-duty hours.

Code of Silence is what Hall (2002) has described in his research on police culture as the perception that police officers will never inform on another police officer in spite of the fact that a police officer may have compromised him/herself.

Completed Suicide as defined by Shneidman (1985) involves the act of taking one's own life.

Critical Incident Stress (CIS) as described by Kureczka's (1996) research on stress in law enforcement denotes a type of stress ensuing from situations which in time become overpowering. Such events are sudden and powerful and fall outside the range of ordinary human experiences. Because they happen so abruptly, Kureczka asserts that they can have a strong emotional impact even upon an experienced and well-trained officer.

Critical Incident Stress Involvement as described in Mitchell and Everly's (1993) research on stress debriefing among emergency service workers, is an all-inclusive support group that interacts accordingly with police officers to assist with issues associated with the emotional elements often caused by stress.

Culture is defined as aspects of human cognition and activity that are derived from what we learn as members of society, keeping in mind that one learns a great deal from what one is never explicitly taught (Monaghan & Just, 2000).

Line-of-Duty Death (LODD) denotes the death of a police officer while on duty. It usually includes, but is not limited to, deaths that are accidental in nature: assaults, crash accidents, duty-related illnesses, shootings, heart attacks, motorcycle accidents, being struck by a vehicle, vehicle pursuit chases, and vehicular assaults, as defined by the Officer Down Memorial Page, Inc. (ODMP, 2009).

Quasi-Suicide denotes attempted suicide with less than total lethality (Shneidman, 1985).

Rookie is a term used by Henry (2004) with respect to a member with limited tenure and experience as a police officer. The probationary period, according to Henry, for a rookie police officer is usually a 1.5 to 2-year process.

Suicide Ideation denotes the consideration of suicide as an option as defined by the American Psychological Association (APA, 2009).

Veteran is a term used to describe an officer who is no longer on probation (Henry, 2004).

The-Thin-Blue-Line is a phrase that symbolically denotes a sense of responsibility by the police officer that separates order from anarchy (Crank, 2004).

Road Warrior denotes a person in a police organization who recognizes the connection between the organization and the police officers who are principally involved in the work of providing public servant duties.

Importance of the Study

It is hoped that this project may yield evidence that could benefit police organizations and management and may shed light and awareness of a police officers' sense of concern with regard to the complex issue of police suicide. Moreover, this research project may provide educational opportunities that address the difficult issue of suicide in police departments and the related mental health issues of depression, stress and or mental illness. The potential for a compulsory preemptive training program could significantly diminish the stigma often connected with the psychological issues associated with suicide among police officers. Kelly (2005) asserts that the recognition of police officer suicide by administrators may provide eligibility for acquiring federal monies for additional training on the issue of police suicides. The conclusions reached in this research project may assist administrators who face the issue of police officers who are prone to depression and who may consider suicide as an option. Overton and Medina (2008) believe that the stigma of mental illness could be minimized by further discussion and exploration of suicide ideation.

Kelly's (2005) research on the incidents of police officer suicide is a subject that is often avoided by many law enforcement departments. Violanti (2007) discovered a propensity by some law enforcement departments to misclassify, misrepresent and or conceal the incidence of a police officer's suicide. Violanti asserts that many law enforcement suicides are often intentionally misclassified. This speaks to what Douglas (1997) has asserted is the lack of attention concerning the prevalence of police officer suicide in this country.

Summary

This chapter provided information on suicide in the law enforcement community. It is hoped by the researcher that this project will add to the existing literature on police officer suicide and help identify factors that could conceivably reduce the number of suicides throughout the law enforcement culture. The Centers for Disease Control (CDC, 2005) has identified suicide as a public health concern. In addition, Satcher (1999) noted that suicide has grown to epidemic proportions in retrospect to the law enforcement community, a further reason to expand research on the topic. Further, Shneidman's (1996) research on the suicidal mind has affirmed that the general increase of suicide rates often happens in an environment or system where the theme of suicide is considered a forbidden subject. This is further compounded by the law enforcement community's tendency to disguise and misinterpret suicide as an accident because of the taboo-like nature of suicide, and in consideration of insurance compensation. By failing to acknowledge the vicarious liabilities shared by police officers and administrators alike, this further promulgates what Clark and White (2003) have asserted that depression and suicide remain virtually "made-up."

Violanti and Samuels (2007) noted that within the very ranks of the law enforcement community, a seemingly negative overtone is oftentimes associated with the suicide of a fellow law enforcement officer (ODMP, 2009). Lejoyeux et al. (2008) have indicated that a significant contributor to law enforcement suicide as a viable option for some is the associated abuse of alcohol and or controlled substance abuse. Waters and Ussery (2007) have also subscribed to this opinion, further asserting that person(s) in general working in high-risk and or high-stress occupations and who are repeatedly exposed to traumatic events throughout their careers, run the risk of making themselves vulnerable to suicide as an option (Violanti, 2007). Cross and Ashley (2004) have put forth the notion that the law enforcement culture continually perpetuates suicide as an option of choice through a series of factors often associated with silence, dishonor and an ubiquitous acceptance of the unwritten code of silence.

CHAPTER TWO: REVIEW OF THE LITERATURE

Introduction

Plumbing police officers' perceptions about suicide may facilitate what Kelly (2005) sees as a means towards developing an effective intervention program that addresses the phenomenon of suicide among police officers. The prevailing absence of consideration and emphasis on identifying the triggers that lead a police officer to consider suicide communicates what Hackett and Violanti (2003) have described as a resounding message to the rank-and-file that suicide is not important enough for consideration by police administrators.

This literature review includes an examination of the past, as well as the current information concerning the perception of police officers with regard to depression and suicide. Cross and Ashley (2004) and Violanti (2007) all assert that an examination of risk factors would be beneficial to more understanding of police suicide. This researcher project examined scholarly works that are relevant to the subject of suicide, with an emphasis on investigating why police officers commit suicide.

The Law Enforcement Culture

Waters and Ussery (2007) have asserted that the law enforcement culture influences an officer's perceptions of incidents of trauma. Prolonged contact with distressing incidents can lead to outcomes that Gray and Lombardo (2004) characterize as making police officers vulnerable and susceptible to the psychological issues associated with suicide among police officers. In addition, Waters and Ussery clarified the importance of the impact of traumatic incidents over a repeated period of time and how they are experienced by police officers. According to Blum (2000), a police officer learns to diminish and even disregard these emotional disturbances, and in so doing insulates him/herself from stressful and traumatic events. Nonetheless, the denial of these emotions, according to Weisinger's (1985) research on anger, makes the officer in fact more susceptible to stress induced psychological disorders. In the absence of support from one's peers, a police officer subsequently learns to maneuver away from what Weisinger describes as any form of dialogue that could conceivably explore their feelings with respect to the traumatic events experienced throughout their career. Cross and Ashley (2004) assert that this reluctance underscores how silence can contribute to an officer's distress, thereby contributing to an increased risk of suicide as a way out.

Hassell's (2006) research on police organizations infers that "culture" is difficult to describe. Hassell defines it is a process that facilitates an appreciation for what Crank (2004) has also described as the behaviors, rituals, and structure that is a distinguishing feature in most law enforcement cultures. Crank moreover advances the notion that it is not something that you can see or even touch, but you can feel it. He further asserts that no other profession is so shielded by a cultural model that is self-justifying as is in the law enforcement community.

According to Triandis (1994), culture is characterized as a group of people who collectively develop for themselves a surviving mechanism that facilitates a process of communication and survival stratagems. This culture aids one another whenever there is an increased level of stress or stressful incidents. Triandis has highlighted the importance of distinguishable social roles that often build trust, along with a sense of commonality at faster rates than Crank (2004) and Violanti (2007) have suggested.

In respect to other professions, law enforcement is an occupation where the penchant for nerve-racking incidents is the norm. Karlsson and Christianson (2003) have characterized police work as an occupation that is repeatedly filled with extended periods of mundane patrolling oftentimes quickly interrupted when an officer must respond to life-threatening incidents in mere seconds. Within the very fabric of the law enforcement culture there is the necessity of highlighting a shared belief system (Quinn, 2005). Quinn further asserts that the hazards associated with law enforcement work regularly attracts individuals who choose a career that draws colleagues closer together; they are often closer with each other than the typical family unit.

Steven's (2005) research on police culture and behavior supports the viewpoint that individuals within the law enforcement community frequently demonstrate a shared value and belief system that defines the make-up of the law enforcement family. Violanti and Samuels (2007) characterize a typical day for an officer as consisting of a host of calls-for-service that regularly deal with situations from traffic, domestic, alarm calls, common incident reports to street level situations, active shooters, assaults, abused children and spouses, natural disasters, terrorism and death. Crank (2004) characterizes these daily interactions as having a noteworthy value in shaping the behaviors and cultural perceptions of a police officer in perpetuating a code of silence (Quinn, 2005). Quinn further asserts that there remains an unwritten rule defining the expectations of an officer, and is often enshrouded in secrecy, away from the public. Frey (2007) also asserts that the code of silence is at best an indiscernible armor of sorts that is connected with the uniform, badge, service firearm, and the authority of the law of the land. Quinn indicates that nonconformity could serve as the grounds for an officer to be expelled and labeled a risk and a subject for corrective action and alienation.

Cancino and Enriquez's (2004) research on police officer peer reprisal for not safeguarding the police culture, has defined the code of silence as a device for sponsoring clandestine conduct that does not jeopardize another police officer. Cultural norms, especially in the law enforcement community, often include a significant amount of isolation and silence, which discourages the need to come forward and seek help (Crank, 2004). It is an unspoken code of conduct about what is accepted within a police culture. A police officer will shelter another officer regardless of the possible punishment. It is an internal system of social control by one's peers in an effort to manage an individual's actions through what Crank describes as peer pressure and the threat of internal retaliation from the rank-and-file. Given this construct, Carter's (1985) research on police perspective and internal control asserts that personal issues are set aside to protect the system and its members as a whole. Reiner's (1978) research revealed that police members eventually label an officer who does not conform to the code of silence negatively and as a possible outcast.

In contrast, Blum (2000) asserts that any exploitation of authority can lead to conduct that is often ubiquitous in law enforcement today. The code of silence can conceivably perpetuate misconduct or deviant behavior for reasons that assures confidentiality to the rank and file. Reiner's (1978) research on the sociological implications of the police persona affirmed that the component of power that is often synonymous with police work frequently invites persons who are in need of and seek power. Quinn (2005) indicates that the code of silence is a pervasive element in the communication process and further perpetuates the sharing of information among officers. Quinn goes on to discuss that information sharing is critical to an officer's survival and is the very essence of the law enforcement culture, oftentimes communicated through stories, anecdotes, and or cynical commentaries about the public and the department. Niederhoffer's (1967) research on the urban police officer stated that officers become notoriously contemptuous about the people they serve and about the inefficiencies of the criminal justice system.

The law enforcement culture is surrounded by symbolism and rituals, as Crank (2004) has asserted, and is often demonstrated and displayed emblematically in the form of a bond through the badge or shield that a police officer wears on his/her uniform. Crank states that the badge is the outward symbolic representation of the law and represents a bond among police officers. According to Blum (2000), the badge symbolizes power.

Black's (1980) research on the conduct of police officers revealed that law enforcement organizations represent social control and self-regulation; its core employs societal conformity and obedience in many situational settings. Ross's (2000) research on the emerging trends in law enforcement assert that police officers and the public maintain a sense of consideration for one another by accommodating to this self-regulating sense of social control.

Law Enforcement and Suicide

Violanti et al. (2006) and Waters and Ussery (2007) have recognized that in the course of the career of a police officer, the many eye-witness accounts to stressful and or traumatic events can have emotional long lasting effects that reach well into the pre- and post-retirement years. The National Police Suicide Foundation [NPSF] (2008) stated that less than 2% of more than 18,000 police agencies have any type of in-service training to address self-care. Kelly and Martin (2006) state that more police officers die by their own hands every year in the United States than are killed on duty. In contrast, Perin's (2007) research highlights the general perception among law enforcement officers that police officers who take their own lives are perceived to be weak in character. Kelly and Martin, as well as Waters and Ussery, have all underscored the perception that depression alone does not necessarily mean that suicide is a long looming possibility. They assert that an officer's predisposition towards considering suicide as an option is compounded by depression-type symptoms, alcohol abuse, substance abuse and a diminished sense of peer support in times of increased and or pervasive stress.

Violanti (2007) asserts that the prevalence of suicide, from the rookie to the veteran police officer, necessitates that a police agency be ever watchful and pro-active in recognizing the signs and symptoms that are often associated with self-destructive behavior. Police administrators are inherently responsible for main-taining a vigilant leadership stance that recognizes that suicide is a factual pro-spect for some police officers who suffer from depression-type symptoms, alcohol abuse, and substance abuse and who have a limited support system in place.

According Violanti (2007, as in all cultures suicidal methods vary, that is to say that how one commits suicide is oftentimes unique and distinctive to the ethos of one's culture. Violanti further affirms that police officers are predisposed to suicide with the use of their assigned on-duty service firearm. An officer's under-standing and familiarity with their own firearm and the consequences of what a self-inflicted injury, makes it the weapon of choice (Violanti). This of course is well documented given the fact that Nagourney's (2007) research on the availabil-ity of guns adequately explains that a significant number of suicide attempts are committed with a firearm. Nagourney goes on to assert that a predictable numbers of suicides are often linked in part to the lethality of the firearm itself. It is im-portant to differentiate the symbolic connotation associated with an officer's as-signed duty weapon as being the sign of their role as a peace officer and enforcer of the law and what Violanti characterizes it as a representational extension of the officer. Violanti notes that the significance of the assigned duty weapon becomes palpably obvious when it is taken away from the police officer. The socialization practices that are unique to the law enforcement community predisposes an officer to a proclivity towards suicide, and suicide becomes an option in times of real or unreal perceived despair and distress.

Law Enforcement and Risk Factors

Pegula's (2004) research on workplace suicides determined that risk factors often associated with police officers make them susceptible to a higher than average level of suicide. Pegula goes on to assert that physiognomies or risk factors often associated with suicide among law enforcement officers include but are not limited to the repeated availability of firearms, alcohol abuse and or substance abuse, as well as a diminished sense of peer support in times of increased or pervasive stress.

Aamodt and Stalnaker's (2001) research on police officer suicide and frequency have sketched out what they have characterized as a typical profile of a police officer who considers suicide as an option: a 30+-year-old male who is Caucasian, with approximately 12+ years of law enforcement experience. This typical profile of a police officer who commits suicide usually does so when in an off-duty status, more often than not using their assigned duty weapon on themselves. The NPSF (2008) has also characterized the police officer who commits suicide as having marriage and family issues, a diminished sense of worth, poor performance evaluation and a recurring contentious pattern of careless behavior on the job.

In exploring further the precipitating risk factors often associated with police officers who commit suicide, the NPSF (2008) asserts that the frequency of officers who take their own lives occurs one out of every 17 hours. Douglas's (1997) research on police suicides suggests that police officer suicides might conceivably be as high as 300+ per year in the United States. Violanti's (2007) work on the clinical and behavioral perspectives of police suicides, as well as the World Health Organization's (2000) research findings, have suggested that many police suicides are often obscured or misclassified as accidental deaths. Much of this misclassification and or concealment are in part due to insurance claims and the corresponding embarrassment that a department or police agency may attract for not having addressed and recognized the sign or risk factors that a police officer who commits suicide may have demonstrated. Kelly and Martin's (2006) research suggests that this purposeful attempt to misclassify or conceal the real death of a police officer makes accurate reporting almost impossible and further stymies any efforts towards recognizing the risk factors of a police officer who commits suicide.

The NPSF (2008) conducted a national survey to look into the various motives as to why police officers commit suicide. The survey revealed that the prevailing reason for police officers who committed suicide was because of a death of a partner or sibling. Other factors included life-threatening medical issues, self-recrimination for some act committed that was deemed injurious to another person, isolation that often led to a self-sequestration from one's peers and significant others, sexual impropriety, arrest or impending indictments, termination, incrimination, and imminent incarceration.

In considering the applicable risk factors involved with respect to why a police officer would commit suicide, Durkheim's (1979) research on the sociological implications of suicide states succinctly that it is deeply rooted in the collective unconscious of a society in general. That is to say, suicide is an individual manifestation of self-enmity and or self-extermination of the individual. Violanti's (1995) research on understanding the surreptitious whys and wherefores for suicide puts forth the clinical prospect that the individual officer may be anguishing or be in despair, suggesting a symptomatic feature that a mental disorder is more than likely to be a causative factor.

It would be prudent for any researcher interested in this subject to not lose sight of what Burke and Mikkelsen's (2007) research on the pervasive features associated with suicidal ideation among police officers has revealed: the law enforcement profession is a dangerous and impenetrable career at best. Waters and Ussery (2007) have pointed out that law enforcement is an occupation that habitually witnesses tragedy and the worst side of humankind daily. Tuck's (2009) research on living on the edge and the integration of spirituality in the law enforcement profession draws attention to the predisposition of a deterioration of the psyche, as well as the decay of the emotional well-being of the officer.

Cross and Ashley's (2004) research on trauma and the dangers of police work underscore the importance of the risk of suicide among what they describe as occupational subcultures. This is pervasive in the law enforcement profession in which a correspondingly high level of stress or distress and social role expectations are overly emphasized. Tate's (2004) research on police suicide and preventative intermediations puts forth the notion that police officers are more likely to consider or commit suicide. This is especially true in the case of wanting to alleviate a career filled with acute life stressors; what Liberman, Best, Metzler, Weiss and Marmar (2002) have coined in their research as the routine occupational stress and psychological distress in police work as a dominant feature of diminishing mental functioning. Heim et al.'s (2009) research on trauma and the risk factors often associated with chronic fatigue syndrome indicate that suicide ideation is an undiagnosed mental disorder that oftentimes result in depression, occupational boundary degeneration, a diminishing sense of self, waning performance job productivity, suicide and homicide. Kelly's (2005) research on mental health and the police professional reveals that depression may be a contributing factor in facilitating a diminishing sense of interconnection with the law enforcement agency and may in fact lead to a real proclivity towards suicide as an option.

Law Enforcement Research Limitations

According to Kureczka (1996), the available literature on suicide within the law enforcement profession is limited. This is due in part to the police officers' reluctance to speak candidly about the type of stress resulting from circumstances that surround the culture; what Burke and Mikkelsen (2007) have asserted as the cultural influences or the rationale for considering suicide. Burke and Mikkelsen further assert that cultural concerns often influence an individual's reason for considering suicide, and Fendrich, Kruesi, Grossman, Wislar, and Freeman (1998) indicate that culture often dictates the manner in which a suicide is accomplished, and in law enforcement it is oftentimes associated with an officer's service weapon.

Police suicide, as Jamison (1999) has asserted precipitates action often resulting from a buildup of a series of critical and at times life threatening incidents throughout a law enforcement officer's career. Jamison further asserts that there is a penchant for a substantial amount of time and energy involved in the planning of a suicide by a law enforcement officer. Hackett and Violanti's (2003) research on tactics for the prevention of police suicide have stated that when closely examined, many risk and warning signs become unmistakably apparent after the death of a police officer. They further state that a rash nature allegedly attached to the act of an officer committing suicide is often linked to the availability of one's assigned duty weapon, allowing for a minimal amount of time for a police officer to reconsider his/her actions.

Summary

Chapter Two began with an investigation of the literature that includes a discussion of the relevant material available on police officer suicide and an officer's perception in considering suicide. An in-depth examination with regard to the role that belief systems and culture play in the law enforcement community was also conducted. A police officer's work is associated with depression, mental illness, and the pervasiveness or absence of peer support which also play a large part in police officer suicide (Waters & Ussery, 2007).

CHAPTER THREE: METHODOLOGY

Research Design

Quantitative research was not suitable for this dissertation since the usage of this type of research model does not afford an in-depth interpretation of the lived experience of the participants. Quantitative design does not facilitate more open communications of the participants (Moustakas, 1994). A phenomenological model was fitting for this project largely because of the potential richness of the participants' perspective on the issue of police suicide. According to van Manen (1990), the use of a phenomenological model on lived experiences facilitates further appreciation of the participants' perceptions, yielding a significant account of collective daily practices. Further, according to Sokolowski (2007), phenomenological research, in an effort to search for personal truths and limits of the participants to be interviewed, is a better instrument for collecting data. A phenomenological method is for that very reason a suitable model in understanding the lived experiences of participants (Moustakas).

Population and Sample Size

The population examined included police officers from the Coral Gables Police Department, which is a local metropolitan police organization in the Miami-Dade County, Florida. Miami-Dade includes a number of police organizations; the population sample was comprised of sworn law police officers only. The area of Miami-Dade includes 4,000+ full-time and part-time officers. Police officers working in the Coral Gables Police Department were contacted using a snowball sampling; all participants will remain anonymous.

The application of content searches used in this dissertation utilized key terminology to pull together as many applicable resources as possible in completing this project. The key words focused on the subjects of depression, firearms accessibility police culture, police stressors, police suicide, police training, mental illness, police organizational administration, PTSD, labels, stress, suicide, and suicidal theory. Given the vast quantity of information on the internet, the author recognized that it was impossible to search every resource; the key word search alone was incomplete and non-comprehensive. The majority of sources for this project were dated between 1999 and 2010 mainly for historical purposes.

Suicide is a complex issue, and is forbidden in a number of cultures and subcultures alike. During the research phase, the author noted a lack of existing research on the subject of police officer suicide, oftentimes believed to be triggered by the inviolable issue of suicide and its complex association with the police community.

Instrumentation

According to Kirk and Miller (1986), the focus of qualitative research is inevitably tied to the implications and practices that an individual places on the phenomena within a shared paradigm and includes narrative stories, behavior, job-related performance, and interactional relationships in common (Moustakas, 1994). Strauss and Corbin (1990) and Moustakas note that qualitative research often comes from a deficiency of available literature. The emphasis of qualitative methods is on open-ended questions; a search of perceptions into the phenomenon that is to be studied (Neuman, 2005). The heart of this research proposal was on the acuity and information that the participants offered, further supporting a qualitative method for this research.

According to Moustakas (1994), the qualities and structure that differentiates qualitative from quantitative investigation is in understanding the importance of the information gathered. For a phenomenological approach to be useful, the emphasis must be on sum of the experience, in spite of the fragments of memory or on the explicit experiences of the participants (Moustakas). The objective of this project was to find implications and practices within experiences, rather than to gather and analyze quantifiable kinds of measurements. By the practice of using a formal and informal interview format, it was expected that this would provide a personal interpretation of the phenomenon of police officer suicide.

Assumptions

It was anticipated that the participants would be truthful and frank in their responses. It was understood that a participant's honesty is a subjective issue at best; that a police officer's interpretations of events and or circumstances may perhaps not reflect the authenticity of an experience (Quinn, 2005). Quinn clarified quite succinctly that police officers form a type of brotherhood among themselves and are often sheltered by a code of silence, and through that code of silence countless police officers develop an attitude toward being disingenuous with outsiders. It is through such duplicity, as Quinn asserts that reality becomes less apparent, and the influence of the code of silence becomes more apparent. Quinn asserts further that slips that would constitute a type of deliberate omission, fabrication, and fraud in incident reports and testimony, when thoughtfully examined in comparison to what in fact is the truth, becomes the weapons of choice of the police officer.

Quinn (2005) notes that the code of silence exerts a controlling influence on a police officer's conduct. They are often reluctant about sharing information, or have trepidation with respect to giving too much information. Disinclination about sharing information may often be the result of what Waters and Ussery (2007) describe as the subject matter itself. The culture of the law enforcement community, as Waters and Ussery have suggested, is generally reluctant to speak about police suicide; the law enforcement culture very often does not fully recognize the issue. Quite the contrary, it encourages police officers and police administrators alike to conceal police officer suicide via the code of silence (Hackett & Violanti, 2003).

Procedures

This qualitative phenomenological research project consisted of nine demographic questions concerning a police officer's perceptions about suicide. Interview questions were open-ended in framework to permit participants the opportunity to provide in-depths answers allowing for universal themes to become known (Tate, 2004). Questions used in the interview stemmed from the existing literature in relation to the reasons why officers choose suicide. Questions were phrased in a manner to achieve an appreciation of the participants' acuity within what van Manen (1990) describes as a phenomenological perspective. The perceptions of police officers involved in this research may provide additional information and awareness of their lived experiences. These experiences may be a causative factor relative to the issue of officers who demonstrate an increased level of stress where individual safety is oftentimes compromised.

Data Processing and Analysis

The intention of this research project was to explore the lived experiences of police officers regarding their acuity with respect to the subject of officer suicides. Taken as a whole, the aim of the data collection was to cultivate a deeper appreciation of the specific lived experiences of police officers and the impact that police suicide has on the law enforcement community in general.

Data were collected via the use of audio-recorded interviews. Prior to the interviews being conducted, the participants were required to read and return a signed informed consent form. In an effort at building a connection, demographic interview questions were asked of each participant. Interviews were completed to the point of reaching data saturation. According to Boyd (2001), data saturation occurs along a continuum that encompasses two to ten participants. Boyd further asserts that fullness or data saturation is not a functionality of the quantity of participants, but rather of discovering the occurrence of universal themes from the information collected.

By interviewing a minimum of 10 police officers, a better perspective about their lived experiences of suicide was obtained. This helped reach a point of data saturation along anticipated common themes (Boyd, 2001). The interviews lasted up to 60 minutes. The time prearranged for each interview made possible an adequate amount of time for the participants to respond to the questions completely and also allowed themes to emerge from the information. Each interview was audio recorded with the consent of each participant.

According to Moustakas (1994), the phenomenological interview is a pre-scribed process of a series of open-ended questions and commentary, and consists of the lived experiences of each research participant. Moustakas further asserts that open-ended questions are asked because they call up deeper commentary and are therefore relevant to this project. Qualitative research adds to the views of the participants via the use of universal or all-encompassing themes (Moustakas). There is a limited amount of literature that exists about the phenomenon of police suicide. Information gathered was pieced together from audio recordings, tran-scripts, and notes. Information was then examined by using NVivo 10® software. Themes were recognized by the number of times each subject was presented throughout the course of the interview.

Ngwenyama (2001) described the phenomenological method rather succinctly with respect to the notion of shrinkage of clustered groups and developing themes. Simply put, it is often accomplished by asking, Does each statement contain something adequate enough to constitute an understanding of itself? That is to say, is it conceivable to diminish further statements without sacrificing the meaning of statements put forth by the participants (Ngwenyama).

Level of Significance

The significance of this research project was to better understand the issues faced by police officers and for presenting them with fitting choices whenever they ex-perience circumstances that could lead them to consider suicide as an option. The contributions made by understanding the concerns that plague police officers over the course of their careers may facilitate a decrease in the number of suicides.

Summary

It is hoped by this researcher the data collected in this phenomenological qualita-tive research project may provide awareness into the complex phenomenon of police suicide. The acuity of influence that a sworn police officer from a munici-pal agency within Miami-Dade County, Florida was explored. This research pro-ject endeavored to appreciate the lived experiences of police officers concerning their perceptions and the far-reaching effects of suicide.

Data was gathered by audio-recorded throughout the interview process and transcribed via the use of NVivo 10® software. According to Violanti and Samu-els (2007), there is a trend that suggests that more law enforcement officers take their own lives than are slain in the line of duty. According to Hackett and Vio-lanti's (2003) research on police suicide, more officers die of self-inflicted wounds than are killed in the line of duty.

Police officers share a distinctive affiliation whereby one may risk their own life for another police officer without any disinclination or question. Crank (2004) asserts that police officers in general recognize the struggles and familiar circumstances of the lives of their fellow police officers, but often do not discuss among themselves these particular circumstances out of respect for their fellow officers and in order to adhere to the code of silence. The code of silence is a set of understood rules of secrecy with regard to questionable conduct by other police officers (Quinn, 2005).

Chapter Three contained a review of the methodology for a phenomenological research approach. Phenomenological research, according to van Manen (1990), allows for a broader appreciation of the lived experiences of the participants. The appropriateness for this research was defined in relationship to the stated problem, purpose, and content examined. It was hoped that the population interviewed would yield information that could facilitate a better understanding of the perceptions and beliefs about the lived experiences of police officers, and may provide awareness into the motives for why an officer would consider suicide.

CHAPTER FOUR: FINDINGS

The purpose of this research project was to explore the perceptions and or consequential effects of police officer suicide. What is provided in Chapter Four is a record of common themes using a methodology originally presented by Moustakas (1994). In addition, this chapter is an in-depth account of the participants' demographics, as well as responses by participants to the interview questions. The population selected included police officers from a local municipal agency (The Coral Gables Police Department) in Miami-Dade County, Florida. The target population included only sworn police officers. Interviews were conducted to explore common themes about the personal experiences of these officers with respect to factors that could feasibly contribute to a police officer considering suicide.

Common themes were collected through a series of interviews, whereby participants responded to nine demographic and nine interview questions. The police officers' interviews were digitally recorded and a transcript was completed in an effort to maintain basic cogency in content. Digital audio recordings, as well as finished transcripts, were reviewed numerous times to determine common themes. The setting of one-on-one interviews and the focus group permitted an atmosphere of confidentiality and an air of privacy and discretion. In general, the acuity for having police officers involved in the research project proved useful in providing awareness of their lived experiences. This contributed to an understanding of the factors that could influence a police officer to consider suicide. The themes were accordingly grouped and further separated by meaning. The emerging themes were evaluated for their textural and organizational contents (Moustakas, 1994). Many of the emerging themes were defined and included verbatim examples from the transcribed interviews of the police officers. Themes were identified using NVivo 10® software (QSR Int., 2012).

Themes were grouped into categories based on major and identifiable patterns. Collection of emerging themes continued until information saturation or information redundancy was reached. The entire interview process lasted approximately one week. Police officer interviews were 20 to 30 minutes. All the interviews met this criterion, with the exception of the focus group interviews, which lasted an hour-and-a-half.

Preliminary Implications

The preliminary suppositions prior to the commencement of this project suggested that there might be factors worth considering with respect to police officer suicides. When considering these factors, common characteristics, such as personality make-up, had to be weighed; there was a possibility that people who have a propensity towards being depressed and stressed may be at risk for suicide (Hackett &

Violanti, 2003; Violanti, 2007). Another consideration was the guarded world view of the police profession which often misclassifies suicide as accidental. Avoiding any shame cast on a police department in the wake of a police officer suicide may lead to such misclassification. In addition, a police department that misclassifies suicide may do so to safeguard a police officer's insurance benefits (Violanti, 1995). Moreover, there is also the suggestion that police officer suicide does not exist, and that there is indeed no crisis (Violanti, 2007).

Demographics

The elevated incidence of suicide among police officers begs the issue that some type of research be conducted and that it focuses on discovering the prevailing inferences associated with this crisis. In comparative studies on police suicide, it was suggested that it might be on the rise (Aamodt & Stalnaker, 2001). Whites occupy more than 80% of all police officer positions and many of these police officers are between the ages of 35 and 54 years of age accounting for the second highest number of suicides in the United States. In consideration of these findings, males comprise 89% of all police officer positions (Aamodt & Stalnaker).

The police officers who participated in this research project were chosen randomly from a participating police department in Miami-Dade County, Florida. The participants consisted of all males, all originating from a segment of the working population deemed to be at a high-risk for suicide (CDC, 2005). The age of the police officers who participated in this research study ranged from ages 46 to 55 years (60%) with the remainder of the respondents ranging from 36 to 55 years of age (40%). Of those respondents who participated, 47% were White, 33% were Hispanic, 13% were African American, and 7% Multi-Cultural in origin. With regard to marital status, 80% were married, 13% were divorced, and 7% were separated from their spouses. The educational make-up of the respondents indicated that 20% had a high school diploma, 40% had an Associate's Degree, 27% had a Bachelor's Degree and 13% had graduate degrees. The length of service of the respondents revealed that 47% had 25 years or more, 13% had 20 years or more, 33% had 15 years or more, and 7% had 10 years or more of continuous service as a sworn police officer.

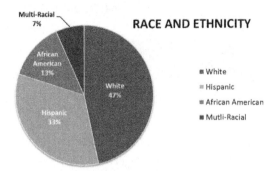

Figure 1: Race and Ethnicity

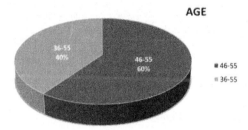

Figure 2: Age

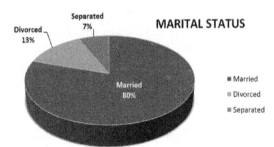

Figure 3: Marital Status

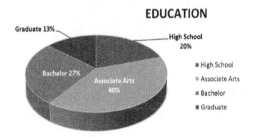

Figure 4: Education

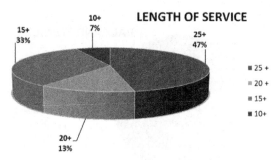

Figure 5: Length of Service

P1	P2	P3	P4	P5	P6	P7	P8	P9	P10	P11	P12	P13	P14	P15
Male	Male	Male	Male	Male	Male	Male	Male	Male	Male	Male	Male	Male	Male	Male
White	Hispanic	Hispanic	White	African Am.	Hispanic	White	Other	African Am.	Hispanic	Hispanic	Hispanic	White	White	White
46-55	46-55	36-45	36-45	36-45	36-45	46-55	36-45	36-45	46-55	46-55	46-55	46-55	46-55	46-55
Married	Married	Married	Married	Divorced	Married	Divorced	Separated	Married	Married	Married	Married	Married	Married	Married
High School	Associate	High School	Bachelor	Associate	Associate	Associate	Graduate	Graduate	High School	Associate	Bachelor	Associate	Graduate	Bachelor
CGPD	CGPD	CGPD	CGPD	CGPD	CGPD	CGPD	CGPD	CGPD	CGPD	CGPD	CGPD	CGPD	CGPD	CGPD
Municipal	Municipal	Municipal	Municipal	Municipal	Municipal	Municipal	Municipal	Municipal	Municipal	Municipal	Municipal	Municipal	Municipal	Municipal
Officer	Officer	Officer	Officer	Officer	Officer	Officer	Lieutenant	Lieutenant	Officer	Sergeant	Officer	Officer	Officer	Sergeant
25+	20+	15+	15+	15+	20+	25+	15+	15+	25+	10+	25+	25+	25+	25+

Figure 6: Demographics

Findings

Suicide claims approximately 30,000 lives each year in the United States (Satcher, 1999). It is especially pervasive within the law enforcement profession (Kelly & Martin, 2006; Violanti et al., 2006). It is projected that more than 300 to 500 police officers commit suicide each year (Kelly & Martin; Violanti et al.). More police officers die by their own hands than are killed in the line of duty, making suicide the number one leading cause of death for police officers nationwide (Violanti et al.).

The purpose of this research project was to explore the perceptions and consequential effects with respect to police officer suicides. Jamison (1999) asserts that the act of suicide is not necessarily a secretive affair, but is often connected with predictably established psychological behaviors often associated with the act itself. This research study yielded the following information on the various themes that subsequently emerged.

Interview Question 1

What type(s) of difficult situations have you or another police officer you have come across in your law enforcement career would lead you to consider suicide as a choice?

Most police officers who participated in this project had not considered the possibility of suicide as a choice; a few cited pending Internal Affairs Investigations into alleged misconduct that could have led to charges or dismissal from the police agency. Some also said that stressful events in their line of work, such as being surrounded by suicide events and environmental factors can all contribute to the possibility of suicide as an option.

Officer P11: "I would imagine, if I killed a kid, if I shot an innocent kid, you know, suicide, yeah, I don't think I ever considered suicide. Yeah, I don't think so."

Officer P13: In response to stressful events, "Twenty-six years, I've done a lot. There is a lot of stress involved here. Outside, it affects a great deal. We've talked about this before. We go to work and there is nothing but stress. You go to work with more stress. There was a point there, when I was on day shift, the one that stuck out, that there were two Latin women who made a left turn on New Year's Eve and they got T-boned by a DUI. Of course, nobody knew, the whole family was at the house celebrating New Year's. I had to go and knock on their door, the door opens, and there's this whole family there, all of a sudden they started screaming and crying the husband walked up to me, he just looked at me, I didn't say nothing. They're dead aren't they? I didn't say anything. How the fuck do you answer that? You see all this stress and shit, and everything else, you see a lot of things, you respond to it, you become cold, cynical, all that shit, but does it mean anything to you suicide? I mean I've been stressed out, depressed, I've seen a therapist, has it gotten to that point, no. Can I see it getting to that point, maybe not for me, based on what we do, maybe not for me, but I can see that happening."

Despite the fact that a majority of the police officers denied the possibility of suicide being an option, it was nonetheless not ruled out as a possibility.

Officer P14: "It never got to that level for me at any point; and Umm, through the good and the bad at work. It never got to that level. There have been some depression and anger, there's been all those feelings, that's the tipping point, it just never got to that point. It doesn't mean that it won't ever, I'm not worried about you guys, I'm worried about you guys getting in your 60s and 70s and then pulling the pin because, you know, because...."

At the core of the matter, there is a prevailing fear about police officers who become so identified with the role of being a police officer that it causes alarm.

Officer P14 stated: "So intertwined in this job, and I worry about these guys, and people who start out being explorers, wanting to become cops, they become cops forever, and in some of our cases, stuff that happened years ago, nonetheless..."

Officer P13 goes on to state: "There is an officer, he was a cop 24/7, he was in the uniform all the time, his kids are away at college, there's is a domestic situation at his home, they become separated in time (husband and wife), he doesn't have a life outside of this. The last time I talked to him, he was separated, living in an efficiency, dude, you've got nobody to blame but yourself. You know, like, the stressors get you, you mention (P12) that officer who had killed himself because of a pending divorce, you throw in a fuckin' medical problem and shit, add financial problems, it's, how well you're put together."

Interview Question 2

In respect to your experience with your present law enforcement organization, what type of in-service educational program did you undertake concerning the topic of suicide?

The majority of the police officers indicated almost nonexistent training or in-service educational program that would address the issue of suicide. It was even suggested that a non-caring attitude of sorts was the predominate message that was communicated by the administration to the police officers department-wide.

Officer P14 stated: "I saw McEvoy (police officer who committed suicide at the police station) two days before, a civilian tried to walk up to the door of the rear of the station, and he says: (McEvoy yells out) "Hey, we're not opened yet." The person looks back, wrong building. That van (automobile where the police officer committed suicide) was littered with cigarette wrappers, coke cans and ashes everywhere. I mean you can tell that he was smoking and he said: "This place doesn't care about the "family man." I said to myself, "something's wrong with this guy." He was having a hard time with child care, and I said, why not put him in an administrative job for the summer, he can still do his 59's (Off-Duty Jobs) with weekends off, and be able to transition and deal with his child care problem.....it will at least get him through the summer. I'm telling you again, I think back, he could have been gunning for somebody in particular....I think he just lost his nerve."

Underscoring the point that a non-existent, in-service educational program concerning the topic of suicide having never been addressed was highlighted by one officer:

Office P2 stated: "Training, Umm, I don't recall that they ever covered that in the Academy, certainly nothing since the Academy. We may have touched it."

The mere fact that suicide prevention has never been stated or even remotely discussed department-wide nonetheless it was emphasized in Officer P3's statement:

Office P3: "It's never been mentioned at all. The first I've ever heard of a question regarding suicide."

Although there was general acceptance and acknowledgement that an EAP (Employee Assistance Program) program existed, its program components and protocols were not known.

Officer P5 stated: "No training but, I'm aware of programs like EAP."

One police officer actually volunteered to attend a training program that barely addressed the issue of suicide among police officers. It was circulated in an online PowerPoint presentation to the department, but was not taken seriously by the rank-and-file. No other known in-service educational program was cited as being available.

Officer P8 who attended the training program stated the following: "Ahh, well, one of the best emotional survival for police officers. Ahh, (referred to a commander in the Department overseeing Special Investigations Section). I volunteered for it many years ago and then in one of the annual training advisory meetings we had I recommended it to senior staff and it was actually implemented as a training course department-wide. It was one of those online things you had to go on, one of those online courses, but it's never about the guys here. It was too expensive, but it did have the whole course online. Everybody did it online. Ahh, one of the classes I went to, one of the best class I went to, talks about the stages of your career and the environment that you work in and the emotional ups and downs as far as the cycle of daily police work."

Officer P15 who is a retired police officer, summed it up by stating: "Preventive training program....when did that come out? (Laughing) When did that come out? (Laughing)."

Interview Question 3

Thinking back on the training you received with your present agency, what could have been done to improve and enhance the efficacy of the suicide education (if any)?

The wide array of responses to this question was as diverse as the police officers who responded, and seemed to echo real problem-solving opportunities. In addition to mentioning that a training program addressing the issue of suicide would be advantageous, there was specific discussion of the fact that improving the lines of communication and developing outreach and human diversity programs would be a vast improvement to the programs that are presently in place.

Officer P1 stated: "To establish a training program, a regular training program, I don't think we have one, I've never seen an established program that deals with that. I know they have one in the military, because of all the military suicides they have. It's a lot of fuckin people. More than people that get killed on the battlefield. As far as I know, they had to establish something before they can improve upon, I would think."

On addressing the issue of improving the lines of communications and developing a human diversity program that would address the issue of suicide:

Officer P4 stated: "What could have been improved? Yes, I remember McEvoy (the Police Officer who committed suicide). No communications. No outreach. No one reached out to him."

The availability and the offering of some type of training would first have to be considered as Officer P2 stated:

Officer P2: "Well, first of all, you have to offer this training; it should be something on a voluntary basis. I think it should at least be offered."

There was of course, some skepticism about the issue of whether any type of training program could have prevented the suicide that occurred.

Officer P3 stated: "I'm sorry (repeat the question)? I don't think it would make a difference usually the question is suicide or suicide attempt? Yeah, anything is good to have a fundamental, Ahh, is that what Crisis Intervention Training (CIT) is? Oh I see. I guess it would help to have some type of understanding, how people are thinking what they're thinking. I know one good real good friend of mine who shot himself, I forgot his last name, it was a steroid issue. They were going to have to amputate his arm; he shot himself with a shotgun. Over, five or six years ago, in fact, it may have been more than five or six years."

A creative solution offered by one of the police officer's was the prospects of first and foremost having an open forum of sorts that would sensibly facilitate discussion on the topic of suicide.

Officer P6 stated: "I think discussing it would be a good idea. Having an open forum where you can tie it into any class you want to tie it where you can have a couple hours of open discussion. As people talk about it. It's a start. I think the department frowns upon it. I personally don't like to go to police funerals, I went to one once, and I swore I would never go to one again. I don't know if it's denial or where it would fall unto, but, Umm, I don't know what it would fall equivalent to. I probably would still not talk about it."

This particular suggestion of having an open forum that would facilitate additional discussion on the topic of suicide was also emphasized:

Office P9: "Well, they should have, I think they should have a class, at least once a year, to talk about the issue, they never talk about it, and, maybe they should have, or be visible and explain how people who have a problem and how easy it is to get therapy. Like I said, talk about it."

An alternative solution to offering a training program to address the issue of suicide was for the department to be proactive in order to prevent the incident that occurred, that is to say, the department intervening and lessening the chances that Officer McEvoy would kill himself.

Officer P7 stated: "Oh yeah, they could have created something. Yeah they could have seen him (Police Officer who committed suicide). They should have taken his gun from him, or put him on administrative leave, or sent him to that guy (psychologist), or that guy would come here and tells him what he should do, I guess not because of confidentiality. I mean I know that's all they do."

A level of frustration was evident in many of the remaining police officers who responded to this question and suggested a matter-of-fact dryness in responses that resonated in one officer's statement:

Office P10: "I guess it would improve if it actually existed. It doesn't. We haven't had any training."

Officer P10 echoed the sentiment of the remaining police officers in minimizing the possible course content of such a preventive training program stating: "That goes to the human diversity shit, touchy, feeling, everything else and all of this shit, Crisis Intervention Training for Baker Act's (Involuntary commitment to a Crisis Unit), nobody touched that, suicide prevention. Stress relations for officers and shit. What's there, oh yeah, stress kills."

There was a real looming fear discussed among the police officers with respect to never having had a preventive training program that addressed suicide and eventual retirement.

Officer P14 stated: "We should be having a program that helps this guy take a position, but they don't. There should be a kind of a program where you hold the door and while he (officer who is in need of help) is going out the door (retirement)."

Interview Question 4

Considering your experience with the agency you are employed with, in what way does your police organization demonstrate concern about your welfare on the issue of suicide?

An overwhelming number of responses to this question suggested a lack of regard for the police officer by the administration. There was a categorical acknowledgment by the majority of the respondents that they all felt that they were disposable and just another number in the organization.

Officer P6 stated: "…everyone has become a number here, and I think, Umm, I think it is across the country, not just here. I think it's just something that is happening across the country. I couldn't talk from experience, but I think it's pretty pervasive."

The collective message that was communicated was one that emphasized a department that was out-of-control and no longer concerned for the welfare of its police officers. A resounding message that many were "hurting" and a lack of concern for the police officers in general was evident.

Officer P2 that asserted: "I don't, I don't see any kind of outward concerns, physical or with mental health, to be honest with you."

Officer P13 echoed the same sentiments and stated: "Stop right there, they don't. Suicide is part of everything that you have to do. As for our agency, you're looked as if you're disposable, you're in the DROP (Retirement Program), and they don't care."

Notwithstanding the fact that an EAP program is available, the prevailing thought by many of the respondents was one of distrust for the system and the overriding belief that no confidentiality existed.

Officer P14 stated: "Let me ask you a question, you, you, and you, who really believes that EAP is really confidential? (Laughter among all the officers in the focus group)."

Officer P12 stated: "I don't think it's confidential at all, but me going to him, Hey, (referring to the psychologist he spoke to), this is what's going on, yes, its confidential. He (Commander) has the sole right to pick up the phone, to call the City Manager or Human Resource to say, take him off the road. It's his obligation."

One of the respondents indicated that in lieu of attending a program, the past common practice of attending choir practice was a means towards helping one another to alleviate the stressors of police work.

Officer P13 stated: "You have to have, you have to have a certain trust, comfort and rapport, you have to have certain, we all have this in common, do you have that with the psychologist, (unintelligible)...that's not going to happen. We used to have a choir practice, with people you know, choir practice was great, because, everybody would "BS," you'd vent, basically it would be a venting session, you'd get it out of your system."

The cynicisms and misgivings that often resonated throughout the interviews bore witness to the fact that many of these police officers were disbelieving of their department and its management staff.

Officer P13 stated quite succinctly: "...it doesn't get better, God forbid if some of these people come forward with their problems, do you think that these young guys can do this? You think that they can do this? Anything can happen."

There was a consistent concern for what many of the respondents felt was a department that was no longer running itself.

Officer P15 stated: "That shit has gotten out of control...right now."

Officer P13: Many of the respondents were in agreement with him as he stated the following: "I mean.....there are people here that you want to take out and beat the shit out of them. You want to tell them, dude, you're fuckin hurting everybody, physically, emotionally, psychologically, department wide, you're killing us."

Officer P15 put forth the opinion that what happened to the department, in retrospect to what he and many of the other respondents echoed, was a sense of loss and embarrassment to a department that they had once held in high esteem. He stated:" It's a shame to what's happened to this place."

Interview Question 5

What efforts do your peers do to diminish the strains that depression often exert on fellow officers who may consider suicide as an option?

For many of the police officers who responded to this question, a uniform response of never having heard of anything to diminish the strains that depression often exerts on fellow officers who may consider suicide was indicated. Many felt that there was no help available; overall, a general feeling of futility was apparent. If any type of preemptive measure was ever taken on behalf of the administration, it was rarely heard of. The indisputable impression from many of the respondents suggested that discussion was not encouraged and in fact discouraged, subsequently sponsoring a behavioral response from police officers to anguish in their own depression, further isolating them from their fellow officers.

Officer P6 stated: "I think it's something that doesn't get discussed. I think that when guys get depressed they get isolated, we isolate them, just talking about that, that officer that we were just talking about, oh yeah, he has lost a lot of weight. We've become so impersonal and I think it has to start somewhere from a leadership role to make things more personal. To reach out; we tend to get away from people we are afraid of. It's sort of like the fear of opening up a Pandora's Box for ourselves. Along with that, we're scared that he may rub off on us. It might open up some wound for us, and say wait a minute; he's no better than I am; maybe something to look at."

If any type of pro-action is taken, it is generally believed to be pointless and ineffective, even harmful to the police officer's ability to keep his job.

Officer P8 stated: "Very rarely any kind of action is taken."

Officer P9 stated: "…they don't talk about it. Nobody talks about it."

In reconsideration of this question of whether there is adequate peer support to diminish the strains that depression exerts on a fellow officer who may be considering suicide, a disconcerting message of non-involvement and denial is unquestionably evident and even inadvertently encouraged by the administration.

Officer P2 stated: "I mean, I haven't seen any obvious attempts to by anybody to, but then again that is something that I don't project that I guess I'm suicidal, I would like to think that, just talking with people, with each other would help somebody in that situation. I don't know really. It happens."

There was little, if any real consensus that peer support was broadly accepted among the respondents; in fact, a broad theme of seeing oneself different from the general population was sponsored. A theme that resonated was of police officers being a breed apart.

Officer P15 stated: "Remember, cops are a different breed than the general public, because, we're more guarded than the general public. We can walk down the street, and you can see that this person is off his rocker, but cops are more guarded, we really have to be more trained in the law enforcement aspects."

Given the fact that an overall accord of non-communication and non-support exists among police officers and the administration, and that nothing is done to encourage a sense of peer support, a feeling of despair is palpable and disserves the department and its officers.

Officer P13 stated: "Nothing has been done. You know, it's like, you keep asking, you keep looking, to all of these questions, everything, it's all symptomatic, the problem is, they use you up. You know, it's not just, they don't' do the minimum of what they have to do. Yeah….that's what, that's what…that's what it all comes down to; for being such an accredited agency, oh my God, this and that, its bullshit!"

Interview Question 6

How do you view the police culture encumbering an officer's ability to look for help on the subject of suicide?

Dealing with the issue of a perceived attitude of superiority associated with what is typically seen as a police officer's world view is a principal thought for concern. Integral to the police image is the compulsion to be seen as a guardian and defender of the law. This is further compounded by the fact that police officers are often seen as the vanguards for perpetuating a standard of conduct that is above and beyond behavioral expectations that most private citizens are unable to achieve. The machismo element is often associated with this perceived attitude of superiority and can be counterproductive, and can also prevent an officer from seeking help. A general attitude of just "sucking it up" is omnipresent in the police culture.

Officer P1 states: "Because it is the culture, that macho culture, you know, you're considered to be a pussy or a weak individual if you're considering suicide, rather than admit to depression, you closet it."

Officer P8 asserts the following: "Ahh, it is still very much a macho environment, so the mere fact that seeing a shrink or psychologist is probably still frowned upon."

The syndrome often associated with being the embodiment of Superman is relatively universal yet feasibly unattainable. It is this notion of believing that one must be stronger and more resilient than the general population further thwarts any possibility of looking for support when needed.

Officer P2 states: "Umm, the culture you know, Superman, you know, kinda ideology, stereotypes, that we have to be stronger than other people."

Given that police officers see themselves apart and above the general population, and that the need to seek assistance and help is viewed as a sign of weakness, it makes sense that embracing this notion of superiority discourages seeking help and reinforces the notion that those that seek help are consequently labeled as mentally ill.

Officer P5 states: "Umm, Umm, I think there is Umm, and overall culture, Umm, and law enforcement, that ah, you know Ahh, that Ahh, how do I want to put this, (pause),Umm, you know, that anyone with mental illness is just labeled crazy. Umm, the term 43 (Police code/signal for someone who is a Baker Act and or mentally challenged), is used loosely, and that Umm, {BR} always them not us."

Added to this is the fear of being perceived as incompetent and weak. For a police officer, this component is not acceptable and daunts any efforts for seeking help on the subject of suicide as a consideration.

Officer P6 states: "I think people reach out so much for help that I think that we see ourselves as if nothing can affect us. So, I think if we were to reach out, I think it would make us incompetent to do the job. Mentally I think we would think now I am incompetent to do the job. I guess here I am helping this person out, but 8 hours ago, I was sitting in a couch. So I think that's why, fear of acknowledging that we are human, and fear that maybe we can't do our job. If we are expressing our issues, whatever issues we have, with a therapists, I think 10 hours later we come here to do our job how am I going to be helping out; it's like an alcoholic stopping a person for DUI. It makes no sense what-so-ever. Why am I even doing it? So, I think that maybe one of the issues."

Officer P11 states: "...you know our personalities, it's just a show of weakness, and so, is that what you're getting at? You don't want to tell anybody that you're having problems."

Promotional advancement is also impaired, should a police officer make public that they are having problems.

Officer P14 states: "If your number one on the lieutenant's list and you reveal to the department that you have a problem, you're not going to get promoted."

The emphasis of surviving in a police environment pressures a police officer to be invisible and consequently susceptible to a host of issues that could conceivably entertain suicide as a means towards alleviating oneself of any emotional concerns that can inevitably become overwhelming in time.

Officer P13 states: "You become invisible" and Officer P14 also asserts the following: "Then you become vulnerable."

Officer P12, in response to being invisible and then vulnerable, makes reference to reference to the following example: "This guy just recently got into a major 34 (signal that denotes a domestic and or quarrel that is ensuing), with a supervisor, and it was swept underneath the carpet because the Major told everybody to do it. I mean, it's well-known, well it's not well known, but the supervisor is aware of it, and when it was brought to my attention, I looked at this certain supervisor, I said, what are you going to do about it? Because if you don't do something about it, then I might, he said I'll take care of it; I'll take care of it. Well, I don't know if it's being taken care of."

Interview Question 7

In respect to your experiences with your present law enforcement organization, what types of training programs have you had that would have addressed the issue of suicidal thoughts?

The overall responses generally stressed that there were no training programs on the issue of suicide. There was only one respondent who did reference a training program geared towards management; the issue of suicide was marginally discussed. This training program was not made available to the rank and file and was not a compulsory training program of the management staff of the department.

Officer P8 stated: "After taking the class, I actually I had a few commander classes where we touch briefly on it but not very much in depth to the training program."

Officer P11 stated: "I'm trying to think if I'd had anything. May not be something that the City puts on, I attended something, no, no, no, and maybe they sent me to a class that I asked for. I'm not saying something that everybody took, and trying to think of some of my classes (long pause), yeah, maybe a command staff course, I took stress management class, it may have mentioned depression or suicide that kind of thing, I don't recall if they told me much about suicide. I can't think of any."

If there was any training program that dealt with the issue of suicide attended by a police officer, it more than likely addressed the issue of suicide in the civilian world instead.

Officer P10 stated: "More dealing with the public than dealing with ourselves."

In retrospect to the suicide that occurred in the department, Officer P1 alluded to the fact that there're may have been a training offered that may not have quite entirely addressed the issue of suicide. He was not able to call to mind the name of the training, but did offer to state the following:

Office P1: "None; well, I've only seen it once within this particular department and they ignored it that was with Tommy Mac (police officer who committed suicide). They just kind of brushed it aside. They didn't really give a shit about it; at least not what I saw."

Another police officer mentioned an in-service class that he could not remember the name of, and was not entirely sure if it (suicide) was in fact ever mentioned.

Officer P2 stated: "…just the services, counseling, whatever."

There was a general consensus that inevitably the only ones a police officer can really count on is themselves, despite the fact that it (suicide) is a subject that is hardly ever spoken about.

Officer P3 stated: "…all we have is our personal life experiences and just common sense I would think to some extent. All we have is each other."

Officer P6 asserted the following: "I can't remember any. I think it would be worthwhile to pursue. Our CIT (Crisis Intervention Training) training may have had a small part or component about suicide, but it must have been a small part, I don't remember. It was nothing about us."

Interview Question 8

How do police supervisors and command staff speak to the issue of police officer suicide in your law enforcement organization?

Once more, there was consensus that the issue of police officer suicide is profoundly nonexistent in the department to police supervisors, command staff and the police officer. Officer P13 gave reference to Officer McEvoy and his suicide stating the following:

Officer P13: "None, we don't. Nobody even talks about it. With McEvoy, nobody mentions his name. When was the last time the department ever mentioned his name?"

One officer indicated what was actually needed to ensure that police supervisors and command staff speak to the issue of police officer suicide.

Officer P1 stated: "Address it to begin with. They need to address it before they can improve or assist on anything until they're willing to address the issue. Tommy Mac, they never addressed the issue, and even after he did it (referring to suicide) The Major of Uniform Patrol had lunch an hour later while the guy was sitting there dead in the back of the station, this person was the Patrol Division Major." "...I don't think that shit has ever been addressed here, or in any police department that I've ever been in. I've never heard of it ever being addressed. It happens, depression, I think depression fuckin rampant in this job. Between personal issues, the shit they (police officers) sees, the financial problems that everyone has, I think the fuckin depression is easily as rampant here if not more so in the civilian population."

The issue of liability for the department was circuitously mentioned, that is to say that a reasonable explanation why a suicide prevention training program for police officers is not offered is because of what is perceived to be the legal burden that a department would invite upon itself, principally, the responsibility to do all that is necessary in identifying and circumventing any possibility that a police officer under duress may consider suicide as an option.

Officer P3 states: "...honestly I don't think they want to know about it because then there is possibly a liability, it's the last thing anyone wants to hear."

Officer P6 asserts: "I think they don't. I think is something that they hope it doesn't happen, there is no preventive maintenance at all, I mean none at all. None, we're definitely not proactive, we're definitely reactive. If there are reactive measures, I don't know what those reaction measures are."

To further clarify the point that police supervisors and command staff do not address the issue of suicide, Officer P9 states the following:

Officer P9: "They don't. They never say one word about it. They don't."

Officer P11 also asserts: "I mean you know it's not something that people will talk about. So I, I don't know."

With respect to actually addressing the issue:

Officer P13: "...we're not putting anything in place that there should be, and really, when you look at it, how hard would it be to put something in place?"

Interview Question 9

How can police supervisors and command staff ward off the risk of suicide as an option for your fellow officers?

A number of recommendations were offered by the respondents with respect to warding off the risk of suicide as an option for their fellow officers. At its basic level, one police officer suggested having informal meetings with people and showing concerns for an officer's family life and how it impacts their work performance. One officer suggested that one should not forget their "root." That is to say, that as one progresses through the ranks, it would be appropriate to remember one's beginning and to not lose sight of the stresses that often wreak havoc on a police officer in the performance of his/her duty.

Officer P3 states: "...Number one, don't forget we're we started, I mean, this is just a job, it's basically a job. Forget about the departmental orders, or administrative policies, what about the human factor, you know, we all make mistakes? They (administrators) want to live by the book, they just want to burn you and make your life miserable, what about us, taking care of us. But as shifts go on, schedule changes we all have families, you know, yet we don't get the credit or appreciation."

Officer P9 also suggested and stated: "Well, I think the supervisors could be more in tune to their subordinates, to see what's going on in their lives. They don't have to get personal, but if they see somebody change a little bit they should get more involved and talk to the person about their problem, and then talk to them about getting help..."

Another suggestion would be to develop programs that have inherent failsafe measures that would adequately address potential suicidal risk for officers.

Officer P4 states: "Programs, talk about it. We have incidents like what happened to McEvoy, why weren't there any failsafe mechanisms to help him. If you think about it, his children, his stress with his ex-wife, going to court, and a shift that didn't work for him, taking care of his children, reference, had to make an appeal to accommodate taking his kids to school, after work, and he couldn't work shift hours given to help pick-up his children, stress on that. Not caring. Ignoring his needs, and coming to the station, and doing the suicide just to make a point......in police work as in other departments, they have suicide prevention, we don't, why not?"

Having supervisors be more acquainted with the signs and symptoms often associated with a police officer considering suicide as an option.

Officer P6 states: "...the front line supervisor should have enough of a keen eye to watch people, to see that they've lost some weight, I mean you can see it, we've seen them here. I don't know if there is something in place, or position to start stepping in. I mean they have procedures when we get contacts (reference complaints from the public) from the public, steps, procedures, do they have that for people who are sick, I don't know. I don't know where we are with that. We should absolutely have that."

In conjunction with recognizing the signs and symptoms often associated with a police officer considering suicide as an option, it would be beneficial for supervisors and police officers alike take training classes that addressed the issue of police suicide specifically. In the process of taking these training classes, Officer P7 asserted:

Officer P7: "They should take these training classes. Oh, no, well, well they should recommend, I want you guys to get this training, we need people to recognize the signs. Right now, I think if they think you're going to commit suicide."

Thematic Synopsis

A review of the information provided by the respondents of this research study resulted in the discovery of five major themes (Fig. 7). They focused on addressing the issue of suicide prevention, talking about the issues of suicide, investing in a training program that would facilitate a broader appreciation for the issues often associated with suicide, identifying available outside resources and a genuine appreciation for the police culture itself. A further discussion of these themes is given in Chapter Five.

As such, thematic outcomes, in general, point towards specific areas that on the surface would appear to be of significant importance to the police officers interviewed. The police culture comprises of a number of major and minor themes when looked at closely. The significance of speaking to this notion of the police culture facilitates an appreciation for the role of the police officer. The police culture on a whole is at the very essence of the thematic results discovered in this research study and demonstrates a noteworthy role in the lives of police officer.

MAJOR THEMES

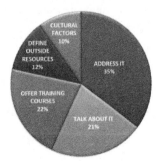

Figure 7: Major Themes

Summary

Chapter Four provided themes that focused on addressing the issue of suicide prevention. It also revealed that suicide was often an option for a police officer who suffered from depression and PTSD. It focused on: (a) addressing the issue of suicide prevention; (b) talking about the relevant issues of suicide as an option for a police officer who may be anguishing in depression, PTSD and despair; (c) inaugurating training programs that would facilitate a broader appreciation for the issues often associated with suicide; (d) delineating available outside resources that could extend beyond the available resources of any police department; and (e) appreciating the make-up and cultural considerations often associated with the law enforcement profession as well as appreciating the extent of its influence among the rank and file.

The research included structural interviews with nine demographic and research questions, which facilitated a structural interview format of the police officers interviewed (Moustakas, 1994). The interviews were digitally recorded and transcribed for better evaluative purposes and included a description, as well as a thorough account of the participants' demographics. The analysis recognized reoccurring and emerging themes that were well supported and justified the detailed responses by the police officers interviewed. Emerging themes were subsequently identified. A cadre of responses was made available through the insights and accounts provided by the police officers interviewed. Voluminous responses provided adequate clarification of a police officer's explanation of the research questions presented.

Chapter Five encapsulates the conclusions arrived at during the course of the project. The primary discussion includes identifying the major themes identified and documented throughout Chapter Four. They also include suggestions for creating training programs that may facilitate a broader appreciation of the issues often associated with suicide. Chapter Five concludes with a general synopsis of study limitations, a broad discussion on the major themes identified and addressed with respect to the subject of police officer suicide. Contained within this summary are recommendations for the law enforcement community and its police officers and recommendations for future research on this penetrating subject of suicide through a 3-phase stage approach.

CHAPTER FIVE: SUMMARY, CONCLUSIONS AND RECOMMENDATIONS

Summary

The purpose of this research project was to explore the lived experiences of police officers concerning their perceptions with respect to the subject of police officer suicide. The target population included only sworn police officers. Interviews were conducted in an effort to explore common themes about the personal experiences of these officers with respect to factors that could feasibly contribute to a police officer considering suicide.

The foremost discussion in Chapter Five includes identifying the major themes that were documented throughout Chapter Four. These themes include: (a) Addressing the issue of suicide prevention, or the lack thereof; (b) Talking about the relevant issues of suicide as an option for a police officer who may be suffering from depression and PTSD; (c) Inaugurating training programs that would facilitate a broader appreciation for the issues often associated with suicide; (d) Delineating available outside resources that could extend beyond the available resources of any police department; and (e) Appreciating the make-up and the cultural considerations often associated with the law enforcement profession as well as appreciating the extent of its influence among the rank and file was subsequently reviewed as well.

Limitations of the Study

Despite the penetrating nature of the research subject, many of the respondents were eager to tell their story. More than a few police mid-managers and first-line supervisors conveyed a sense of uneasiness with respect to the subject of police suicide, yet despite this, many wanted to participate. Consideration of a future research follow-up on this same topic merits a broader range of participants. There were no real fears about being unavoidably identified, despite the safeguards that were put in place to protect the identities of the respondents. Many of the respondents were veteran police officers who were already in the process of eventually stepping down and looking forward to retirement. The remaining police officers interviewed had a considerable number of years under their belt. Although a wealth of themes were obtained in this research study, future research would do well to explore police suicide prevention programs along a continuum where empirical data is examined for their effectiveness in application (Clark & White, 2003).

A review of the information provided by the respondents of this research study resulted in the emergence of five major themes. They focused on addressing the issue of suicide prevention, talking about the issues of suicide, investing in training programs that would facilitate a broader appreciation for the issues often associated with suicide, identifying available outside resources, and a genuine appreciation for the police culture itself.

Conclusions

Themes

Theme 1: Address the issue.
Unlike other professions, police work is often besieged with a superfluity of emotional and physical hazards that play havoc on a police officer's life. Police officers are repeatedly faced with violence, vehicular crashes, natural disasters and natural and premeditated deaths. Shift work and the long hours of driving often extoll a heavy price on police officers and their families alike. The outcomes are startling, with more than average divorce rates and separations, suicides, domestic violence, heart disease, higher than normal levels of cancer, depression and alcohol abuse. Waters and Ussery (2007) further expand on the idea that while not everyone in a hazardous profession exhibits noticeable symptoms of stress, the snowballing impact of stress unchecked exacts a price on a police officer. Clark and Haley (2007) and Liberman et al. (2002) asserted that the profession of law enforcement is a dangerous and arduous occupation.

There is a prevailing misconception in the media and with the public that encourages a kind of urban legend that police officers can ward off stress and distress associated with the jobs without experiencing any ill effects. Reuss-Ianni's (1999) seminal work on the effects of police work shows quite the opposite; that is, an ample amount of research has suggested that when stressors are prolonged enough and overwhelming, a person's ability to cope becomes problematic at best. Reuss-Ianni goes on to state that the effects of police work has consistently been a source for experiencing high levels of stress in light of the element of danger, violence, and pervasive health issues that often ensue well beyond the years of service.

The issue of police suicide is one that is often avoided and not talked about by police officers and department administrators. For many police officers, it is difficult, if not awkward, to comprehend why someone would elect to end their life. Confusion and incredulity are typically the first reactions to learning that a fellow officer has committed suicide. There was a general consensus that the issue of police officer suicide is profoundly nonexistence in the department to police supervisors, command staff and the police officers.

Officer P13 gave reference to Officer McEvoy and his suicide stating the following: "None, we don't. Nobody even talks about it. With McEvoy, nobody mentions his name. When was the last time the department ever mentioned his name?"

One officer indicated what was actually needed to ensure that police supervisors and command staff speak to the issue of police officer suicide.

Officer P1 stated: "Address it to begin with. They need to address it before they can improve or assist on anything until they're willing to address the issue.

To further clarify the point that police supervisors and command staff do not address the issue of suicide:

Officer P9: "They don't. They never say one word about it. They don't."

The ability to finally put to rest the notion that police suicides do not affect the rank and file begs that the issue be acknowledged and addressed accordingly. A department that recognizes and addresses this issue can put into place an in-service training program that would facilitate recognizing a police officer who may be experiencing difficulties. Encouraging an open-forum and dialogue can be helpful and supportive in assisting a fellow police officer through challenging situations. Formalizing an in-service training program that encourages addressing the issue of police suicide can facilitate a greater sense of self-assurance for the police officer. It would require courageous leadership in a department's management to stand up and say it is time to address the issue of suicide in law enforcement.

Part of the process of creating an atmosphere that adequately addresses the issue of police suicide would involve raising levels of awareness and the risk factors that are often associated with suicide and mental health issues in law enforcement. A culture of support and understanding that could help identify and evaluate existing resources, best practices, and training related to suicide prevention, intervention, and response programs could be explored. In addition, creating a strategic plan to guide police administrators at all levels of the department in mitigating the risk of suicide could only be beneficial. Openly promoting awareness and resources that facilitate an appropriate response that emphasizes the importance of having a suicide preventive program is an integral part of a police officer safety continuum.

Theme 2: Talk about suicide.

The way a person feels inside is critical in obtaining an accurate pulse as to where they are emotionally. It can be actually quite difficult to repress one's feelings, whether sad, worried, or distressed. For many of the respondents, the issue of repression around the issue of suicide, and keeping one's feeling locked inside is not a desirable thing. Nevertheless, talking with someone who cares can lead to one starting to feel better; a person is no longer alone with their problems. It does not mean that the problems and worries magically disappear, but at least someone else knows and can help explore solutions.

Some police officers are more private than others. This means some people are more reluctant about sharing their feelings. An officer does not have to share everything, but it is important to share feelings when one is in need of support.

The opportunity to speak freely without the fear of any repercussions from the department calls for an avenue that is free from condemnation or reprisal. When a department loses one of its own to suicide, the need to process and talk freely about what occurred is very important.

The opportunity to talk without restrictions about the relevant issues of suicide for a police officer who may be anguishing in depression, PTSD and despair, would facilitate a broader appreciation for the issues often associated with suicide

Officer P9 also suggested and stated: "Well, I think the supervisors could be more in tune to their subordinates, to see what's going on in their lives. They don't have to get personal, but if they see somebody change a little bit they should get more involved and talk to the person about their problem, and then talk to them about getting help…"

Another suggestion would be to develop programs that have inherent failsafe measures that could adequately address potential suicidal risk for officers.

Officer P4 states: "Programs, talk about it. We have incidents like what happened to McEvoy, why weren't there any failsafe mechanisms to help him. If you think about it, his children, his stress with his ex-wife, going to court, and a shift that didn't work for him, taking care of his children, reference, had to make an appeal to accommodate taking his kids to school, after work, and he couldn't work shift hours given to help pick-up his children, stress on that. Not caring. Ignoring his needs, and coming to the station, and doing the suicide just to make a point……in police work as in other departments, they have suicide prevention, we don't, why not?"

Officer P6 stated: "I think discussing it would be a good idea. Having an open forum where you can tie it into any class you want to tie it where you can have a couple hours of open discussion. As people talk about it. It's a start. I think the department frowns upon it. I personally don't like to go to police funerals, I went to one once, and I swore I would never go to one again. I don't know if it's denial or where it would fall unto, but, Umm, I don't know what it would fall equivalent to. I'd probably still not talk about it."

This particular suggestion of having an open forum to facilitate additional discussion on the topic of suicide was also emphasized by one officer:

Office P9: "Well, they should have, I think they should have a class, at least once a year, to talk about the issue, they never talk about it, and, maybe they should have, or be visible and explain how people who have a problem and how easy it is to get therapy. Like I said, talk about it."

One successful program that facilitated an opportunity for police officer to talk freely and openly about the issue of suicide was a program developed by the New York Police Departments Early Intervention Unit (NYPD, EIU, 2011). This program integrated many of the tenants of the Army's Teammates Care about Teammates Initiative Program through the practice of a peer counseling initiative. All New York police officers are taught to identify the signs and symptoms often associated with suicide, such as depression, PTSD, alcohol abuse, and recognizing idioms known as suicidal keywords (NYPD, EIU). Police officers are encouraged to persuade fellow police officers to seek professional mental health resources within their community.

An auxiliary component to the New York Police Departments Early Intervention Unit (NYPD, EIU, 2011) employs volunteer police officers trained to recognized the signs and symptoms of suicide through a program affiliated with the New York Professional Police Association, or as it is referred to as the Police Organization Providing Assistance (POPPA). This program has met with great success in stemming the tide of police suicides and integrates peer counseling facilitated by trained police officers to augment the professional services that a qualified clinician versed in suicide prevention provides. The concept is relatively simple: a police officer who exhibits all the potential signs and symptoms for being at risk for suicide are immediately identified. They are subsequently provided the assistance needed to feel that they have alternatives and the ability to talk freely without warranting any repercussions from the department.

Another program that has demonstrated success in curbing suicide considerations and has been met with great enthusiasm among police officers is the State of New Jersey's Cop2Cop (2011) Law Enforcement Suicide Prevention Program. It too has been credited with substantially reducing suicide and with facilitating an environment that encourages the ability to talk seriously about the issue of suicide. New Jersey's Cop2Cop is one of the few programs that have actually demonstrated success in reducing the number of police officer suicides in the State of New Jersey.

Cop2Cop (2011) is more than just a suicide prevention program, it is a preemptive type program staffed by police officer volunteers, both active and retired who work in collaboration with mental health professionals, many of whom were former police officers themselves. It operates 365 days a year, 24 hours a day (New Jersey, DHS, 2010). A key component to the success of Cop2Cop is linked to the dedicated proactive stance taken by the program in training, and for offering services to police officers who may need a forum to talk and to be heard. Cop2Cop offers uniform in-service training to all police departments in the State of New Jersey. It incorporates a state approved suicide prevention program designed specifically for police officers and their families. Consequently, when an incident ensues that involves a police officer who may be at risk anywhere in the State of New Jersey Cop2Cop, police peer counselors are called in by police administrators and field commanders as standard operating procedure to traumatic incidents in the field. The mental health professionals and police peer counselor volunteers are specifically trained to identify and address the typical symptoms associated with the stresses of a police related injury or death (New Jersey Department of Health Services, 2010). Components of this successful program integrate the U.S. Air Forces' (2010), eleven suicide prevention initiatives that identify at-risk personnel, and the U.S. Army's "Teammates Care about Teammates" peer counseling program. Together, these two components serve the interest of preventing police officer suicide. The Cop2Cop's program offers increased resource availability in funding, personnel and administration along a statewide level of operations.

Theme 3: Offer training courses.

The single most lethal aspect of police work is suicide. Some estimates indicate that the suicide rate for police officers can be as much as is 2 to 3 times that of the general public. And three times as many police officers kill themselves compared to those killed by criminals while they are in the line of duty (Nagourney, 2007).

The majority of the police officers indicated an almost nonexistent training or in-service educational program that would address the issue of suicide. One officer highlighted that no in-service educational program concerning the topic of suicide having never been addressed.

Office P2 stated: "Training, Umm, I don't recall that they ever covered that in the Academy, certainly nothing since the Academy. We may have touched it."

Officer P15 who is a retired police officer summed it up by stating: "Preventive training program....when did that come out? (Laughing). When did that come out? (laughing)."

Officer P1 stated: "To establish a training program, a regular training program, I don't think we have one, I've never seen an establish program that deals with that. I know they have one in the military, because of all the military suicides they have. It's a lot of fuckin people. More than people that gets killed on the battlefield. As far as I know, they had to establish something before they can improve upon, I would think."

In support of offering a training program to address the issue of suicide, it is important to take into consideration that police officers are routinely exposed to an array of stressful events. The consequence of doing nothing and not providing a training program not only harms the police officer, but also resonates throughout the department among the rank and file. Moreover, a police officer who commits suicides dies only once, but the spouses, significant others and siblings grieve for the rest of their lives.

The fact remains, police officer suicide continues at a rate much higher than that of the general population. Shneidman's (1996) research on the suicidal mind has affirmed that the general increase of suicide rates often happen in an environment or system where the theme of suicide is considered a forbidden subject. The lack of acknowledging the vicarious liability shared by police officers, and administrators alike associated with the impression of what actually constitutes depression and suicide within the law enforcement organization further promulgates what Clark and White (2003) have asserted in their research on clinicians, cops and suicide as a common misnomer that both concepts remain virtually made-up:

If anything is clear by the responses of our research study respondents, police departments need to rethink their failed and sometimes non-existent attempts on instituting applicable suicide interventions through appropriate training programs. A police officer, who is near the end of their threshold of coping, will eventually lose sight as to what is important to them anymore. Police administrators cannot lose sight of the fact that a police officer whose mind is on other problems, be they at home or at work, is a danger to themselves and to other police officers who may be relying on them. (p. 123)

A new mind set is needed in law enforcement, once and for all, that is not just about police suicide; for every police officer who contemplates and sooner or later commits suicide, there are a hundred more police officers who are still working and suffering from the inherent dangers of the job. There are also hundreds of police officers who do not contemplate suicide as an option; but still struggle with a host of issues brought on by the job. Many of these, such as depression, PTSD, marital issues and alcohol and or drug abuse or some other form of stress are significant enough to alter and disrupt their lives.

The National Police Suicide Foundation puts fourth a first-rate training program that puts emphasis on critical incident stress management, PTSD and a host of other stress-related issues that highlight suicide prevention as its core platform of training. Identifying the signs and symptoms that may lead a police officer to consider suicide as an option requires breaking down the wall of silence and responding appropriately with the resources needed to circumvent any self-harm. The program also underscores the importance of developing standard operating procedures and training programs that will facilitate a police department to take proactive measures in addressing the issue of police suicide.

Any type of training program offered that addresses the issue of police suicide should include an understanding of the dynamics of suicidal behavior. Recognizing the signs and symptoms of a police officer who may be in immediate risk to commit suicide, adopting a voluntary police officer peer support programs, encouraging police officers at risk to seek professional assistance, and not just when a problem arises, but before a problems develop.

For some time now, traditional trainings have only reinvented and repackaged the same traditional suicide programs, peer support and intervention programs in an effort to avert suicides from being considered or happening. In their time, these outdated programs were adequate; however, they no longer serve the best interest of today's modern police officer. The numbers alone prove it. Police suicides are on the rise each year. Even a police department that elects to ignore or hide the numbers can no longer afford the liability.

The issue of liability for the department was circuitously mentioned, that is to say that a reasonable explanation why a suicide prevention training program for police officers is not offered is because of what is perceived to be the legal burden that a department would invite upon itself.

Officer P3 states: "...honestly I don't think they want to know about it because then there is possibly a liability, it's the last thing anyone wants to hear."

Officer P6 asserts: "I think they don't. I think is something that they hope it doesn't happen, there is no preventive maintenance at all, I mean none at all. None, we're definitely not proactive, we're definitely reactive. If there are reactive measures, I don't know what those reaction measures are."

The Badge of Life Foundation established the Emotional Self-Care (2012) program to address the issue of police suicide prevention. The program is more than just a police suicide prevention program. It is a totally new and innovative approach that offers a distinctive and creative suicide prevention training program that emphasizes bringing up issues that may be troubling a police officer. This program helps to determine how things functioning daily for the police officer. It explores and looks for areas of concern where a police officer may want change. Additionally, the program examines a police officer's coping skills to determine if they are healthy or not.

Another innovative and well received training program on police suicide prevention is one offered by the Institute of Police Technology and Management. Its core program offers an appreciation and understanding of the historical roots to how most police departments responds to a police suicide. It evaluates the array of stresses in police work. It identifies and profiles the suicidal police officer and offers ways on how to handle a suicidal police officer as well. Communication skills in dealing with a suicidal police officer as well as developing standard operating procedures and community resources are reviewed. In addition, the Institute of Police Technology and Management program emphasizes a proactive line of management level training that also benefits police officers affected by the suicide of a fellow officer and their family. The program involves training for all police officers, line supervisors and command staff, and union representatives as well as establishing a volunteer helpline. Outcome measures comprise of evaluating suicide rates, pre and post assessments of learning, focus groups, interviews, and follow-up as needed.

Theme 4: Define outside resources.

A review of the information provided by the respondents of this research study resulted in the need for identifying available outside resources that could extend beyond the available resources for a police department. Prevention, awareness, and intervention, outline specific steps that police officers can take to help themselves or someone to recover from a crisis.

Violanti (2003) asserted that when a police officer runs out of coping techniques he will very often contemplate suicide. Regrettably, suicide is a permanent coping solution that some police officers are predisposed to use when caught up in life event's that cause undue stress for themselves (Moore, 2004). While there can be no doubt that life can often get in the way of feeling good about oneself, this is no more truer than as is often the case with police officers who despite the complexities of their profession are still required to perform their duties. Even though police officers have a duty to perform their job, one must keep in mind that while it is admirable to protect and serve others, one must remember to take care of oneself. Trying to balance everything in life can be challenging and demanding at times. It is crucial that police officers explore different means towards managing those challenges effectively through wellness programs.

Police officers must also come to grips with the fact that asking for help will not result in punitive action from their police department, and that all information will be confidential; and those resources available are here to help them deal with their problems. All police personnel, including civilian and management must know the signs of depression and suicide and what to do if they see themselves or another co-worker in need. A number of outside resources are available for police officers and would include the following:

1. 1000 Deaths: Is an outreach source of support sponsored by SOLOS (Survivors of a Loved One's Suicide). This on-line community offers support and healing for anyone who has lost a loved one to suicide. Their mission is that no SOLOS need be alone in grief. http://www.solossa.org/

2. AFSP (2377): Telephone: 212.363.3500. www.afsp.org. American Foundation of Suicide Prevention. Toll Free: 1.888.333. http://www. afsp.org.

3. Cop Shock: Researched for six years, CopShock - Surviving Posttraumatic Stress Disorder (PTSD) reveals how to prevent or manage dangerous PTSD symptoms that can destroy a police officer's career and family life. Family Education Program-Orientation to police functions, problems in police marriages, methods for effective communication, and the family as a source of support.

4. Law Enforcement Wellness Association, Inc: http://www.cophealth. combooklet has been designed to provide information about suicide

5. National Center for Police Officers with PTSD, provides an On-Line resource center and crisis hot-line for police officers, families and friends on PTSD issues. They also provide treatment referrals, court case information, headlines, and informative links. http://www.ptsd.va.gov/ professional/toolkits/toolkits_list.asp

6. National P.O.L.I.C.E. Suicide Foundation: 1.866.276.4615. www.psf.org. The mission of the National P.O.L.I.C.E. Suicide Foundation is to provide suicide awareness and prevention training programs and support services that will meet the psychological and spiritual needs of emergency workers and their families. http://serveprotect.wordpress.com/ tools/national-p-o-l-i-c-e-suicide-foundation/

7. National toll free hotlines operating 24 hours a day, 7 days a week: 1.800.SUICIDE (7842433). 1.800.273.TALK (8255)

8. Peer Counseling: Peer counselors are officers trained to provide emotional support and make referrals when needed. This can involve access to peer counselors in other departments. Peer counselors are volunteers serving on their own time.

9. Pre-retirement Counseling: Officers should be prepared for the difficult transition to life away from "the job" well before their departure from active duty.

10. Professional Counseling: This can be in the department, the union, or the community. Independent sources may be most practical. Referrals to local behavioral health agencies should be available.

11. Stress Education Program: Stress recognition, techniques of physical exercise, proper nutrition, interpersonal communication methods, and coping styles.

12. Suicide: Org: Suicide Prevention, Awareness, and Support http//www. suicide.org/policesuicidepreventionandawareness.html

13. Tears Of A Cop: Resources for additional links to websites providing education and awareness, counseling and support. http://www. tearsofacop.com/

14. The Badge of Life: Psychological Survival for Police Officers http://www.badgeoflife.com.

Theme 5: Cultural factors.

Culture, according to Monaghan and Just's (2000) research on the anthropology of social and culture is defined as aspects of human cognition and activity that are derived from what we learn as members of society. One must keep in mind that a person also learns a great deal that is never explicitly taught. Cross and Ashley (2004) put forth the notion that the law enforcement culture in and of itself, continually perpetuates suicide as an option of choice through a series of factors associated with silence, dishonor and an ubiquitous acceptance in an unwritten code of silence (Cross & Ashley).

A review of the information provided by the respondents of this research study demonstrated a genuine appreciation for the police culture itself. The significance of speaking to this notion of the police culture facilitates an appreciation for the role of the police officer. The police culture on a whole is at the very essence of the thematic results discovered in this research study and demonstrates a noteworthy role in the lives of police officer.

The machismo element of conduct is often associated with this perceived attitude of superiority and as such, can be counterproductive and encumber an officer to seek help. A general attitude of just sucking it *up* is omnipresent in the police culture.

Officer P1 states: "Because it is the culture, that macho culture, you know, you're considered to be a pussy or a weak individual if you're considering suicide, rather than admit to depression, you closet it."

Officer P8 asserts the following: "Ahh, it is still very much a macho environment, so the mere fact that seeing a shrink or psychologist is probably still frowned upon."

The syndrome often associated with being the embodiment of Superman is relatively universal and feasibly unattainable. It is this notion of believing that one must be stronger and more resilient than the general population that further thwarts any possibility of looking for support when needed.

Given this acknowledgment that police officers see themselves apart and above the general population, and that the need to seek assistance and help is viewed as a sign of weakness. It makes sense that embracing this notion of superiority discourages seeking help and reinforces the notion that those that seek help are consequently labeled accordingly as mentally ill.

Officer P5 states: "Umm, Umm, {BR}, I think there is Umm, and overall culture, Umm, and law enforcement, that ah, you know Ahh, that Ahh, how do I want to put this, (pause),Umm, you know, that anyone with mental illness is just labeled crazy. Umm, the term 43 (Police code/signal for someone who is a Baker Act and or mentally challenged), is used loosely, and that Umm, always them not us."

Added to this is the fear of being perceived as being incompetent and weak. For a police officer, this component is not acceptable and daunts any efforts towards seeking help on the subject of suicide.

When considering the particular subculture that is often characteristic of the law enforcement community, there is what Burke and Mikkelsen (2007) have described as an inherently omnipresent nature of the profession. Kelly (2005) and Violanti et al. (2006) have described this as a profession that perpetuates an increased level of tension and distress that facilitates the threat of suicide as a real possibility. Tate's (2004) research on suicide revealed that the rate of suicide in the United States for police officer follows a trend that proportions it at a higher frequency than the general population.

It is important to recognize that all organizations (especially police organizations) have an integral culture that influences the behavior of its members. By far, many of these cultures act within the limits of serving the operational goals of an organization or police department. For the most part, they have a positive influence on the operations of any department. In the case of a police organization, adhering to a code of silence that extends a sense of disproportionate loyalty to other police officers can be counterproductive with respect to addressing the issue of suicide as a consideration for a police officer (Cross & Ashley, 2004). In reviewing the code of silence, Hall (2002) describes in his research on the police culture that it embodies the perception that police officers whether real or unreal will never inform on another police officer, in spite of the fact that police officers may have compromised themselves.

Cross and Ashley (2004) further go on to assert that understanding the police culture is a critical component towards appreciating a police officer's behavior and attitude. The culture portrays the general public as being unsympathetic, not trustworthy, and in some cases, possibly a threat. In order to maintain this disposition; an element of secrecy, reciprocal backing, and unity on the part of one's fellow police officer is required. Waters and Ussery (2007) have also subscribed to this opinion in their research that the inherent uncertainty of police work, in combination with the need for control, hints towards a mindset that what Cross and Ashley have identified as a shared mutual dependency that is rooted in this distinctive culture.

Understanding the existence of the distinctiveness of the organizational make-up of the police culture, necessitates acceptance of its own core values, beliefs, and norms that are unique to the profession; and in so doing, acknowledging the influence it has on the police department. In doing so, these values, beliefs, norms, rituals, and expectations are subsequently passed along through the organizational culture early in the new police officer's career. A new police officer is often taught by a seasoned veteran police officer to ignore the training given in police academy (Cross & Ashley, 2004).

Officer P2 highlighted a non-existent, in-service educational program concerning the topic of suicide having never been addressed who stated: "Training, Umm, I don't recall that they ever covered that in the Academy, certainly nothing since the Academy. We may have touched it."

The mere fact that suicide prevention has never ever been stated or even remotely discussed department-wide, nonetheless there was a prevailing factor and emphasized in *Officer P3's* statement: "It's never been mentioned at all. The first I've ever heard of a question regarding suicide."

Chapter Summary

Chapter Five summarized the results that were identified during the course of conducting the individual and focus group interviews. The discussion included: (a) addressing the issue of suicide prevention; (b) talking about the relevant issues of suicide as an option for a police officer who may be anguishing in depression, PTSD and despair; (c) inaugurating training programs that would facilitate a broader appreciation for the issues often associated with suicide; (d) delineating available outside resources that could extend beyond the available resources of any police department; and (e) appreciating the make-up and the cultural considerations often associated with the law enforcement profession as well as appreciating the extent of its influence among the rank and file. In addition, appreciating the make-up and the cultural considerations often associated with the law enforcement profession, as well as appreciating the extent of its influence among the rank and file is crucial.

Recommendations

A department that recognizes and addresses the issue of police suicide can put into place an in-service training program that would facilitate recognizing a police officer who may be experiencing difficulties. Encouraging an open-forum and dialogue can be helpful and supportive in assisting a fellow police officer through challenging situations. Formalizing an in-service training program that encourages addressing the issue of police suicide can facilitate a great sense of self-assurance for the police officer.

The opportunity to speak freely without the fear of any repercussions from the department, calls for a climate that is free from condemnation or reprisal. When a department loses one of its own to suicide, the need to process and talk freely about what occurred warrants talking about their feelings. The opportunity to talk would facilitate a broader appreciation for the issues often associated with suicide

A new mind set is needed in law enforcement, once and for all, that is not just about police suicide; for every police officer who contemplates and sooner or later commits suicide, there are a hundred more police officers who are still working and suffering from the inherent dangers of the job. It is important to recognize that many police officers who do not contemplate suicide as an option. However, there are those who struggle with issues brought on by the job, such as depression, PTSD, marital issues and alcohol and or drug abuse or some other form of stress that is significant enough to alter and disrupt their lives.

Even though police officers have a duty to perform their job, one must keep in mind that while it is admirable to protect and serve others, one must remember to take care of oneself. Trying to balance everything in life can be challenging and demanding at times. It is crucial that police officers explore different means to-wards managing those challenges effectively.

Police officers must also come to grips with the fact that asking for help will not result in punitive action from their police department, and that all information will be confidential; and those resources available are here to help them deal with their problems. All police personnel, including civilian and management must know the signs of depression and suicide and what to do if they see themselves or another co-worker in need, and recognize the fact that there are outside resources available for them.

The significance of speaking to this notion of the police culture facilitates an appreciation for the role of the police officer. The police culture on a whole is at the very essence of the thematic results discovered in this research study and demonstrates a noteworthy role in the lives of police officer. It is important to recognize that all organizations, especially police organizations have an integral culture that influences the behavior of its members. By far, many of these cultures act within the limits of serving the operational goals of an organization or police department. For the most part, they have a positive influence on the operations of any department. In the case of a police organization, adhering to a code of silence that extends a sense of disproportionate loyalty to other police officers can be counterproductive with respect to addressing the issue of suicide as a consideration for a police officer (Cross & Ashley, 2004).

Quinn (2005) asserts that there remains an unwritten rule that is unspoken, defines the expectations of an officer, and is often enshroud in secrecy from the public. Frey (2007) also asserts that the code of silence is at best, an indiscernible armor of sorts that is connected with the uniform, badge, service firearm, and the authority of the law of the land. Quinn further asserts that nonconformity could serve as the grounds for an officer to be expelled and labeled a risk and a subject to corrective action, and alienation.

Cancino and Enriquez's (2004) research on the qualitative study of police officer peer reprisal for not safeguarding the police culture has defined the codes of silence as a device for sponsoring clandestine conduct that does not jeopardize another police officer from public scrutiny. Cultural norms being what they are, especially in the law enforcement community as stated by Crank (2004) often included a significant amount of isolation and silence from the general public, which discourages the need to come forward and seek help. It is an unspoken code of conduct about what is accepted within a police culture. A police officer will shelter another police officer in whatever situation, regardless of the possible punishment. It is an internal system of social control by one's peers in an effort to manage and individual's actions through what Crank describes as peer pressure and the threat of internal retaliation from the rank-and-file. Given this construct, Carter's (1985) research on a police perspective and internal control asserts that personal issues are set aside to protect the system and its members from the inquiry of the public eye. Reiner's (1978) research revealed that its police members eventually label an officer who does conform to the code of silence negatively. Ross's (2000) research on the emerging trends in law enforcement assert that police officer and the public maintain a sense of consideration for one another by accommodating to this self-regulating sense of social control.

Consideration with respect to establishing a mutual duality between the public and the police obliges the maintenance of an open dialogue that addresses the issues of stress, depression, and suicide shared by both. According to Yang (2003), broadening the baseline knowledge of both the public's perception of the police produces understanding and discovery; and with that, knowledge changes perceptions through improved dialogue and communications. Police officers must open up the lines of communication with their peers and with the public in a hope of warding off miscommunications and inaccuracies about their role and the affect that suicide has on each other.

In an effort at improving their image with the public, informal contacts that show the public police officers as human beings can have a positive impact. The public recognition of the prolonged contact to distressing incidents that police officers are routinely subjected to, often leads to positive outcomes. Gray and Lombardo (2004) have described this as an essential appreciation of a police officer's continual vulnerability to prolonged and intense issues connected with their profession. In addition, Waters and Ussery (2007) further clarified the importance of recognizing the issues and inherent significance that traumatic incidents play and how they are experienced by police officers, and how ephemeral those experiences can be in response to adverse events.

Acknowledging that a problem exists is a necessary ingredient to addressing the issue of suicide among police officers. The lack of recognition that a problem exists communicates to the police officer that the issue of police suicide is not worth pursuing; it communicates a message that police officers are not worthy of any consideration. There was acknowledgment by the majority of the respondents that they all felt that they were disposable and just another number in the organization. Police administrators would do well to remember that they too were once officers and to think about the stress they once faced themselves.

Officer P6 stated: "...everyone has become a number here, and I think, Umm, I think it is across the country, not just here. I think it's just something that is happening across the country. I couldn't talk from experience, but I think it's pretty pervasive."

A police officer suggested that one should not forget his roots. That is to say, that as one progresses through the ranks, it would be appropriate to remember one's beginning and to not lose sight of the stresses that often wreak havoc on a police officer in the performance of his/her duty.

Officer P3 states: "...Number one, don't forget where we started, I mean, this is just a job, it's basically a job. Forget about the departmental orders, or administrative policies, what about the human factor, you know, we all make mistakes? They (administrators) want to live by the book, they just want to burn you and make your life miserable, what about us, taking care of us. But as shifts go on, schedule changes we all have families, you know, yet we don't get the credit or appreciation."

Officer P9 also suggested and stated: "Well, I think the supervisors could be more in tune to their subordinates, to see what's going on in their lives. They don't have to get personal, but if they see somebody change a little bit they should get more involved and talk to the person about their problem, and then talk to them about getting help..."

The ability to appreciate the importance of changing the mindset of a police officer about the inherent stigma often attached to the issue of police suicide necessitates tearing down barriers. Overton and Medina (2008) and Violanti et al. (2006) assert that this lack of recognition of the problem is emblematic of the police culture. Reducing the stigma attached to issues related to depression, PTSD, marital issues, alcohol and or drug abuse or other forms of stress involves providing acceptable channels for police officers to feel safe enough to seek out help for themselves.

The law enforcement profession is a highly stressful occupation; the inherent stress that is part of this profession takes a toll on the body, mind, and spirit over time. Only when administrators begin to relate to their officers by opening lines of communication can this issue be addressed.

Three-Phase Protocol

A three-phase protocol for addressing the issue of police suicide should include the following:

Phase 1.

Development of a plan of action to increase public awareness and training programs on a department-wide level that would facilitate better communication with police officers who are considering suicide. This could be achieved by implementing a suicide prevention program that provides an opportunity for police officers to talk freely and openly about the issue of suicide. Such a model program was developed by the New York Police Departments Early Intervention Unit (NYPD, EIU, 2011). This program integrated many of the tenets of the Army's Teammates Care about Teammates Initiative Program. These programs are recognized as models of excellence. In addition, sponsoring a public initiative program, as well as awareness and information days tailored for police officers and administration alike, should be considered. The model incorporated by the National P.O.L.I.C.E. Suicide Foundation provides suicide awareness and prevention training programs that are measurable and serve populations at increased risk for suicide, such as police officers.

Phase 2.

Endorse a more active and systematic environment that would sponsor suicide prevention planning, implementation, and evaluation on a department-wide level. Shneidman's (1996) research on the suicidal mind has affirmed that suicide often happens in an environment or system where the theme of suicide is considered a forbidden subject. This is further compounded by the tendency for law enforcement organizations to disguise and misinterpret suicide as an accident because of the taboo nature of suicide and in consideration of insurance compensations. Expanding the efforts to provide effective follow-up care could encourage better choices for police officers at risk for suicide.

The importance of developing standard operating procedures and training programs that define a police department's proactive measures with regard to police suicide should be encouraged. Waters and Ussery (2007) have asserted that person(s) in general working in high risk and/or high stress occupations who are repeatedly exposed to traumatic events throughout their careers run the risk of suicide; Violanti (2007) concurs with this concept. Evaluating and assessing present practices could bring awareness of the issue of police suicide. Quinn (2005) asserts that information sharing is critical to an officer's survival.

Phase 3.

Increasing efforts to integrate a suicide prevention program that addresses the issue of substance abuse prevention and treatment services is another consideration in the development of a preventive training program. Waters and Ussery (2007) concluded that substance and alcohol abuse are major contributors of police officer suicide. Evaluating the dimensions of a program on the subject of police officer suicide prevention, in conjunction with available outside mental health services, is another consideration. Such a program could address the mental health issues of depression, stress and mental illness in general, and could help diminish the label often connected with the psychological issues associated with suicide among police officers. In promoting such a program, volunteer police officer peer counselors could be used to provide emotional support and make referrals when needed. Peer counselors are volunteers serving on their own time. An auxiliary component to the New York Police Departments Early Intervention Unit (NYPD, EIU, 2011) employs volunteer police officers trained to recognize the signs and symptoms of suicide. This program is known as the Police Organization Providing Assistance (POPPA). This program has met with great success in stemming the tide of police suicides and integrates peer counseling by trained police officers who are both active and retired. This applied program could augment the professional services that a qualified clinician versed in suicide prevention could provide.

Volunteer police officer peer counselors could also provide services to the bereaved families of police officers who attempt or successfully commit suicide. Such a program could help identify effective methods to mitigate the psychological effects often associated with police officers suffering from unrelenting stress, stress that can make them candidates for suicide. Burke & Mikkelsen (2007), Kelley (2005), and Violanti, Castellano, O'Rourke, and Paton, (2006) all assert that those police officers who are often exposed to repeated distressing incidents over time consider suicide. Violanti's (2008) work on the issue of police suicide revealed that the continual, demanding and distressing situations encountered by police officers can lead to psychological issues. Police officers suffering from unresolved issues, as Kelly (2005) has asserted, in time risk their ability to make sound judgment decisions, and in for making appropriate choices on the job, as well as in their private lives.

Concluding Remarks

The purpose of this dissertation was to explore the lived experiences of police officers with regard to their perceptions and or consequential effects of police officer suicide. The ability to finally put to rest the notion that police suicides do not affect the rank and file should be acknowledged and addressed accordingly. According to Kelly's (2005) research findings, the law enforcement profession is a hazardous occupation. Consequently, a significant number of police officers die in the line of duty each year (ODMP, 2004 thru 2010). Of significance within that length of time, police officer suicides average over 300 per year, contributing to what O'Hara's (2009) research concluded as a significant increase in law enforcement deaths nationwide. Waters and Ussery (2007) have also found that substance and alcohol abuse, as well as marital issues, are major contributors of police officer suicide.

This dissertation examined the awareness levels of police officers from a local metropolitan agency in Miami-Dade County, Florida. These officers contributed substantially to understanding the probable factors that mental health plays on police officers, as well as the level that stress plays when personal safety is an issue. A convenient random sample of participants was selected from the Coral Gables Police Department.

The research yielded information that could benefit police organizations and management and also shed light and awareness of a police officer's concern with regard to the complex issues of police suicide. Furthermore, this study revealed that practical education by way of a suicide preventive program that successfully addresses the issue of suicide would be enthusiastically accepted if offered.

The law enforcement culture influences an officer's perceptions of repeated exposure to trauma. Gray and Lombardo (2004) state that prolonged contact to distressing incidents can lead to adverse outcomes. Their research suggests that life events, in conjunction with the stresses associated with the law enforcement profession, have a potential for promoting vulnerability that can make police officers susceptible to suicide ideation. Burke and Mikkelsen (2007) suggest that the law enforcement profession is a dangerous and impenetrable career at best, and Waters and Ussery (2007) have pointed out that law enforcement is an occupation that habitually witnesses tragedy and the worst side of humans daily.

Any training program that addresses the issue of police suicide should include an understanding of the dynamics of suicidal behavior. Such a program should consist of the following: (a) recognition of the signs and symptoms exhibited by a police officer who may be at immediate risk for suicide; (b) adopt a voluntary police officer peer support program; and (c) encourage police officers at risk to seek professional assistance and not just when a problem arises, but before a problem develops.

REFERENCES

Aamodt, M. G., & Stalnaker, N. A. (2001). Police officer suicide: Frequency and officer profile. In D.C. Sheehan & J. I. Warren (Eds.), *Suicide and law enforcement.* Quantico, VA: U.S. Department of Justice.

American Foundation of Suicide Prevention. (2010). *What's new at AFSP?* Retrieved January 26, 2010, from http://www.afsp.org.

Atkinson, J. M., & Heritage, J. (Eds.) (1984). *Structures of social action: Studies in conversation analysis.* Cambridge, UK: Cambridge University Press.

American Psychological Association. (2009). *APA government relations: Science policy.* www.apa.org/ppo/science/.

Andrew, M. E., Hartley, T. A., Mnatsakanova, A., et al. (2008). Suicide in police work Exploring potential contributing influences. *American Journal of Criminal Justice, 34*(1), 41.

Bertolote, J. M., Fleischmann, A., DeLeo, D., & Wasserman, D. (2004). Psychiatric diagnoses and suicide: Revisiting the evidence. *Crisis, 25*(4), 147-155.

Black, D. (1980). *Manners and customs of the police.* New York, NY: Academic Press.

Blum, L. N. (2000). *Force under pressure: How cops live and why they die.* New York, NY: Lantern Books.

Boyd, C. O. (2001). Phenomenology: The method. In P. L. Munhall (Ed.), *Nursing research: A qualitative perspectives (3rd Ed.).* Sudbury, MA: Jones & Bartlett.

Burke, R. J., & Mikkelsen, A. (2007). Suicidal ideation among police officers in Norway. *Policing: An International Journal of Police Strategies and Management, 30*(2), 228-236.

Burke, R. J., & Mikkelsen, A. (2007). Suicidal ideation among police officers in Norway. *Policing: An International Journal of Police Strategies & Management, 30*(2), 228-236.

Cancino, J. M., & Enriquez, R. (2004). A qualitative analysis of police peer retaliation: Preserving the police culture. *Policing: An International Journal of Police Strategies & Management, 27*(3), 320-340.

Carter, D. L. (1985). *Police brutality: A model for definition, perspective, and control.* In A. S. Blumberg, & E. Niederhoffer (Eds.), The ambivalent force (pp. 148-156). New York, NY: Holt, Rinehart, and Winston.

Center for Disease Control and Prevention [CDC]. (2005). *Suicide: Facts at a glance.* www.cdc.gov/ncipc/dvp/suicide/SuicideDataSheet.pdf

Clark, D. W., & White, E. K. (2003). Clinicians, cops, and suicide. In D. P. Hackett, and J. M. Violanti (Eds.), *Police suicide: Tactics for prevention.* Springfield, IL: Charles C. Thomas.

Cop2Cop: Division of the New Jersey Mental Health Services Division (2011). Retrieved on February 14, 2011 from http://www.state.nj.us/humanservices/dmhs/disaster/responder/cop2co

Crank, J. P. (2004). *Understanding police culture (2nd Ed.)*. Cincinnati, OH: Anderson Publishing.

Creswell, J. W. (2005). *Educational research: Planning, conducting, and evaluating quantitative and qualitative research (2nd ed.)*. Upper Saddle River, NJ: Prentice-Hall.

Cross, C. L., & Ashley, L. (2004). *Police trauma and addiction: Coping with dangers on the job.* FBI Law Enforcement Bulletin, *73*(10), 24-32.

DePaulo Jr., J. R., & Horvitz, L. A. (2002). *Understanding depression: What we know and what you can do about it.* Hoboken, NJ: John Wiley & Sons.

Diamond, D. (2003). Departmental barriers to mental health treatment: A precursor to police officer suicide. In D. P. Hackett and J. M. Violanti. *Police suicide: Tactics for prevention.* Springfield, IL: Charles C. Thomas.

Douglas, R, (1997). *Death with no valor.* Pasadena, MD: Keener Marketing Inc.

Durkheim, E. (1979). *Suicide: A study in sociology.* New York, NY: The Free Press.

Emotional Self-Care (ESC) Program (2012). *The badge of life.* Retrieved on June 30, 2013 from http://www.policesuicidestudy.com/id5.html

Fendrich, M., Kruesi, M. J. P., Grossman, J., Wislar, J. S., & Freeman, K. (1998). Police collection of firearms to prevent suicide: Correlates of recent turn-in experience. *Policing: An International Journal of Police Strategies and Management, 21*(1), 8-21.

Frey, A. (2007). *Blue wall of silence perceived in police force.* Retrieved December 05, 2007, from www.dailybulletin.com/news/ci_3503381

Gray, M.J., & Lombardo, T.W. (2004, January/March). Life event attributions as a potential source of vulnerability following exposure to a traumatic event. *Journal of Loss and Trauma, 9*(1), 59-72.

Hackett, D. P. (2003). Suicide and the police. In D. P. Hackett and J. M. Violanti (Eds.), *Police suicide: Tactics for prevention.* Springfield, IL Charles C. Thomas.

Hackett, D. P., & Violanti, J. M. (2003). *Police suicide: Tactics for prevention.* Springfield, IL: Charles C. Thomas.

Hassell, K. D. (2006). *Police organizational cultures and patrol practices.* New York, NY: LFB Scholarly Publishing.

Hall, G. (2002). *A brief discussion of police culture and how it affects police response to internal investigations and civilian oversight.* http://www.cacole.ca/Resource%20Library/Conferences/2002 %20Conference/2002%20Presentations/Hall,%20R.%202002.pdf.

Heim, C., Nater, U. M., Maloney, E., Boneva, R., Jones, J. F., & Reeves, W. C. (2009). Childhood trauma and risk for chronic fatigue syndrome: Association with neuroendocrine dysfunction. *Archives of General Psychiatry, 66*(1), 72-80

Henry, V. E. (2004). *Death work: Police, trauma, and the psychology of survival.* New York, NY: Oxford University Press.

Jamison, K. R. (1999). *Night falls fast: Understanding suicide.* New York, NY: Random House.

Kappeler, V. E., Sluder, R. D., & Alpert, G. P. (1998). *Forces of deviance: Understanding the dark side of policing (2nd Ed.).* Prospect Heights, IL: Waveland Press, Inc.

Karlsson, I., & Christianson, S. A. (2003). The phenomenology of traumatic experiences in police work. *Policing: An International Journal of Police Strategies and Management, 26*(3), 419-438.

Kelley, T. M. (2005). Mental health and prospective police professionals. *Policing: An International Journal of Police Strategies & Management, 28*(1), 6-29.

Kelly, P., & Martin, R. (2006). Police suicide is real. *Law and Order, 54*(3), 93-95.

Kirk, J., & Miller, M. L. (1986). *Reliability and validity in qualitative research.* Beverly Hills, CA: Sage Publications.

Kureczka, A. W. (1996). Critical incident stress in law enforcement. *FBI Law Enforcement Bulletin, 65*(2/3), 10-16.

Lejoyeux, M., Huet, F., Claudon, M., Fichelle, A., Casalino, E., & Lequen, V. (2008). Characteristics of suicide attempts preceded by alcohol consumption. *Archives of Suicide Research, 12*(1), 30-38.

Liberman, A. M., Best, S. R., Metzler, T. J., Weiss, D. S., and Marmar, C. R. (2002). Routine occupational stress and psychological distress in police. *Policing: An International Journal of Police Strategies and Management, 25*(2), 421-439.

Mitchell, J. T., & Everly, G. S. (1993). *Critical incident stress debriefing: An operations manual for the prevention of traumatic stress among emergency services and disaster workers.* Ellicott City, MD: Chevron.

Monaghan, J., & Just, P. (2000). *Social & cultural anthropology: A very short introduction.* New York, NY: Oxford University Press.

Moore, D. C. (2004). *The impact of occupational stress and the effectiveness of stress coping strategies on marital relationships of police officers.* Dissertation, Capella University.

Moustakas, C. (1994). *Phenomenological research methods.* Thousand Oaks, CA: Sage Publications.

Nagourney, E. (2007, April 17). *At risk: Availability of guns raises suicide rates, study finds.* http://www.nytimes.com/2007/04/17/ health/17risk.html

National Police Suicide Foundation. (2008). *Introduction: Understanding the problem is key.* Baltimore, MD: Author.

[The] National Police Suicide Foundation (n.d.). *The enemy within: Police suicide awareness training.* Retrieved on June 30, 2013 from http://www.psf.org/index.html

Neuman, W. L. (2005). *Social research methods: Qualitative and quantitative approaches (6th Ed.).* Boston, MA: Allyn and Bacon.

New Jersey Department of Health Services. (2010). *Health topics A to Z.* Retrieved on January 31, 2011 from www.state.nj.us/health

New York Police Department Early Intervention Unit (NYPD EIU). Retrieved on January 30, 2013 from http://www.nyc.gov/html/nypd/html/employee_assistance/confidentiality.html

Ngwenyama, O. (2001). *Doing phenomenological research.* http://www.cs.aau.dk/~pan/phd-doc/Phenomenological-Research.ppt

Niederhoffer, A. (1967). *Behind the shield: The police in urban society.* Garden City, NY: Anchor Books.

O'Hara, A. (2009). *Police suicide numbers and the chicken little factor.* http://www.policesuicideresearch.com/id4.htm

Officer Down Memorial Page, Inc. (2004). *Honoring officers killed in the year 2004.* http://www.odmp.org/year.php?year=2004&Submit=Go

Officer Down Memorial Page, Inc. (2005). *Honoring officers killed in the year 2005.* http://www.odmp.org/year.php.year?= 2005&Submit=Go

Officer Down Memorial Page, Inc. (2006). *Honoring officers killed in the year 2006.* http://www.odmp.org/year.php?year=2006&Submit=Go

Officer Down Memorial Page, Inc. (2007). *Honoring officers killed in the year 2007.* http://www.odmp.org/year.php?year=2007&Submit=Go

Officer Down Memorial Page, Inc. (2008). *Honoring officers killed in 2008.* http://www.odmp.org/year.php?year=2008&Submit=Go

Officer Down Memorial Page, Inc. (2009). *Honoring officers killed in 2009.* http://www.odmp.org/year.php?year=2009&Submit=Go

Officer Down Memorial Page, Inc. (2010). *Honoring officers killed in 2010.* http://www.odmp.org/year.php?year=2010&Submit=Go

Overton, S. L., & Medina, S. L. (2008). The stigma of mental illness. *Journal of Counseling and Development, 86*(2), 143-151.

Pegula, S. M. (2004). *An analysis of workplace suicides*, 1992-2001. Washington, DC: U.S. Bureau of Labor Statistics.

Perin, M. (2007). Police suicide. *Law Enforcement Technology, 34*(9), 8.

Police Organization Providing Police Assistance (POPPA, 2010). Retrieved on March 4, 2011 from: http://www.poppainc.org

Police Suicide Prevention Program. *Institute of Police Technology and Management.* Retrieved on June 30, 2013 from http://iptm.org/Default.aspx.

Quinn, M. W. (2005). *Walking with the devil: The police code of silence.* Minneapolis, MN: Quinn and Associates.

Reiner, R. (1978). *The blue-coated worker: A sociological study of police union-ism.* New York, NY: Cambridge University Press.

Ross, D. L. (2000). Emerging trends in police failure to train liability. *Policing: An International Journal of Police Strategies and Management, 23*(2), 169-193.

Satcher, D. (1999). *The surgeon general's call to action to prevent suicide 1999.* Washington, DC: United States Public Health Service.

Schafer, J. A. (2008). Effective police leadership: Experiences and perspectives of law enforcement leaders. *The FBI Law Enforcement Bulletin, 77*(7), 13-19.

Shneidman, E. S. (1985). *Definition of suicide.* New York, NY: Wiley and Sons.

Shneidman, E. S. (1996). *The suicidal mind.* New York, NY: Oxford University Press.

Sokolowski, R. (2007). *Introduction to phenomenology.* Cambridge University Press.

Stevens, M. (2005). *Police culture and behavior.* http://faculty.ncwc.edu/mstevens/205/205lect02.htm

Strauss, A., & Corbin, J. (1990). *Basics of qualitative research: Grounded theory procedures and techniques.* Newbury Park, CA: Sage Publications.

Tate, T. (2004). *Police suicide-What can be done?* http://www.tearsofacop.com/police/articles/tate.html.

Triandis, H., (1994). *Culture and social behavior.* New York, NY: McGraw-Hill.

Tuck, I. (2009). On the edge: Integrating spirituality into law enforcement. *FBI Law Enforcement Bulletin, 78*(5), 14-21.

U.S. Air Force Suicide Prevention Program (2010) Retrieved on November 3, 2012 from http://afspp.afms.mil/idc/groups/public/documents/webcontent/knowledgejunction.hcst?functionalarea=AFSuicidePreventionPrgm&doctype=subpage&docname=CTB_018094&incbanner=0

U.S. Public Health Service. (1999). *The surgeon general's call to action to prevent suicide.* Washington, DC: Author.

van Manen, M. (1990). *Researching the lived experience: Human science for an action sensitive pedagogy.* Albany, NY: State University of New York Press.

Violanti, J. M. (1995). The mystery within: Understanding police suicide. *The FBI Law Enforcement Bulletin, 4,* 19-23.

Violanti, J. M. (2007). *Police suicide: Epidemic in blue (2nd Ed.).* Springfield, IL: Charles C. Thomas.

Violanti, J. M. (2008). Police suicide research: Conflict and consensus. *International Journal of Emergency Mental Health, 10*(4), 299-308.

Violanti, J. M., & Samuels, S. (2007). *Under the blue shadow: Clinical and behavioral perspectives on policed suicide.* Springfield, IL: Charles C. Thomas.

Violanti, J. M., Castellano, C., O'Rourke, J., & Paton, D. (2006). Proximity to the 9/11 terrorist attack and suicide ideation in police officers. *Traumatology, 12*(3), 248-254.

Waters, J. A., & Ussery, W. (2007). Police stress: history, contributing factors, symptoms, and interventions. *Policing: An International Journal of Police Strategies & Management, 30*(2), 168-188.

Weisinger, H. (1985). *The anger workout book.* New York, NY: Quill.

World Health Organization [WHO]. (2000). *Preventing suicide: A resource for media professionals.* Geneva, Switzerland: Department of Mental Health.

Yang, B. (2003). Toward a holistic theory of knowledge and adult learning. *Human Resource Development Review, 2*(2), 106-129.

APPENDICES

Appendix A: Consent Form

Consent Form Argosy University

Informed Consent: Participants 18 years of age and older

Dear _____

My name is Michael J. Alicea and I am a student at Argosy University where I am working on a doctoral degree in Counseling Psychology (Ed.D.). I am conducting a research titled: **POLICE SUICIDE: ACUITY OF INFLUENCE.**

The purpose of this research is to explore the lived experiences of police officers concerning their perceptions and or consequential effects with respect to the subject of police officer suicides. The population to be selected will include law enforcement officers from a local municipal agency (The Coral Gables Police Department) in the County of Miami-Dade, in the State of Florida. Miami-Dade County includes municipal agencies as well as county law enforcement officers. The target population will include only sworn law enforcement officers; and as such, a snowball sampling would be completed that would not identify any of the participants in the final research report.

Your participation in the research is voluntary. If you choose not to participate or to withdraw from the research at any time, you can do so without penalty or loss of benefit to yourself. The results of the research may be published, but your identity will remain confidential and your name will not be disclosed to any outside party.

In the research, there are no foreseeable risks to you except the casual possibility of an increased level of stress due to the sensitive nature of the topic being researched. Although there may be no direct benefit to you, a possible benefit of your participation is a contribution to existing and future research about law enforcement suicide.

If you have any questions concerning the research, please call me at 305.525.2482 or 786.222.7671 or you may email at: mjalicea@bellsouth.net or at mjalicea@stu.argosy.edu.

As a participant in this research, you should understand the following:

1. You may decline to participate or withdraw from participation at any time without consequences.
2. Your identity will be kept confidential.
3. Michael J. Alicea, the researcher, has thoroughly explained the parameters of the research and all of your questions and concerns have been addressed.
4. If the interviews are recorded, you must grant permission for the researcher, Michael J. Alicea, to digitally record the interview. You

understand that the information from the recorded interviews may be transcribed.

5. The researcher will structure a coding process to assure that anonymity of your name is protected.
6. Data will be stored in a secure and locked area. The data will be held for a period of no more than 3 years and then destroyed.
7. The research results will be used for publication.

"By signing this form you acknowledge that you understand the nature of the research, the potential risks to you as a participant, and the means by which your identity will be kept confidential. Your signature on this form also indicates that you are 18 years old or older and that you give your permission to voluntarily serve as a participant in the research described heretofore."

Signature of the interviewee: _____ Date: _____

Signature of the researcher: _____ Date: _____

APPENDIX B: DEMOGRAPHICS

Data collection will consist of individual interviews where research participants would be asked 9 demographic and nine interview questions. The intimate setting allows for privacy, which may contribute to participant honesty. Perception of police officers involved in the research may provide insight and knowledge of their lived experiences contributing to potential issues of mental health and mental stability of officers that display increased levels of stress in times where personal safety is compromised.

Do not place your name. Please answer the questionnaire below to the best of your abilities. All information will be kept in confidence.

1. Gender: ☐ Female ☐ Male (please check one)

2. Race and or Ethnicity: _____

3. Age:
   ☐ 25 or younger   ☐ 36 – 45   ☐ 56 – 65
   ☐ 26 – 35   ☐ 46 – 55   ☐ 66 or older

4. Current Marital Status:
   ☐ Divorced   ☐ Now married   ☐ Widowed
   ☐ Never married   ☐ Separated

5. Education: Highest Degree Held

   _____

6. Employment:
   Are you a sworn law enforcement officer with the Coral Gables Police Department in the State of Florida, in the County of Miami-Dade?
   ☐ Yes ☐ No (please check one).

7. What type of law enforcement agency are you employed with?
   ☐ State ☐ County ☐ Municipal Agency

8. What title do you hold with your employing agency?
   ☐ Police Officer ☐ Sergeant ☐ Lieutenant ☐ Major
   ☐ Assistant Chief ☐ Chief of Police

9. How many years have you been a sworn law enforcement officer?
   ☐ Less than 5 years   ☐ More than 5 years   ☐ 10 years or more
   ☐ 15 years or more   ☐ 20 years or more   ☐ 25 years or more

APPENDIX C: OPEN-ENDED INTERVIEW QUESTIONS

The open-ended interview questions utilized in this research include the following:

1. What type(s) of difficult situations have you or another police officer have you come across in your law enforcement career that would lead you to consider suicide as a choice?

2. In retrospect to your experience with your present law enforcement organization, what type of in-service educational program did you undertake concerning the topic of suicide?

3. Thinking back on the training you received with your present agency, what could have been done to improve and enhance the efficacy of the suicide education (if any)?

4. Considering your experience with the agency you are employed with, in what ways does your police organization demonstrate concern about your welfare and on the issue of suicide?

5. What efforts do your peers do to diminish the strains that depression often exert on fellow officers that may consider suicide as an option?

6. How do you view the police culture encumbering an officer's from ability to look for help on the subject of suicide?

7. In retrospect to your experiences with your present law enforcement organization, what types of training programs have you had that would have addressed the issue of suicidal thoughts?

8. How do police supervisors and command staff speak to the issue of police officer suicide in your law enforcement organization?

9. How can police supervisors and command staff ward off the risk of suicide as an option for your fellow officers?

APPENDIX D: FOCUS GROUP

Uncovering the knowledge, experiences, and perceptions of police officers with respect to the prevalence of suicide among officers would be beneficial in recognizing the signs and symptoms that could lead them in considering suicide as an option. This research proposal will explore the perceptions of police officers from a local municipal agency in the County of Miami-Dade, in the State of Florida. Police officers will be appropriate for the research because the Centers for Disease Control (CDC, 2005) classified police officers as being a "*high-risk*" population with a high propensity rate for suicide. Male police officers are more likely to commit suicide than the general civilian population counterparts are and are twice as likely to commit suicide as their female counterparts (CDC, 2005).

During this interview I will be asking you questions that will help me in determining the lived experiences concerning the incidence of suicide among law enforcement officers? The interview will be recorded with an audio recording device. Do you have any questions before we begin the interview?

1. What type(s) of difficult situations have you or another police officer have you come across in your law enforcement career that would lead you to consider suicide as a choice?
2. In retrospect to your experience with your present law enforcement organization, what type of in-service educational program did you undertake concerning the topic of suicide?
3. Thinking back on the training you received with your present agency, what could have been done to improve and enhance the efficacy of the suicide education (if any)?
4. Considering your experience with the agency you are employed with, in what ways does your police organization demonstrate concern about your welfare and on the issue of suicide?
5. What efforts do your peers do to diminish the strains that depression often exert on fellow officers that may consider suicide as an option?
6. How do you view the police culture encumbering an officer's from ability to look for help on the subject of suicide?
7. In retrospect to your experiences with your present law enforcement organization, what types of training programs have you had that would have addressed the issue of suicidal thoughts?
8. How do police supervisors and command staff speak to the issue of police officer suicide in your law enforcement organization?
9. How can police supervisors and command staff ward off the risk of suicide as an option for your fellow officers?

APPENDIX E: CODING SHEET: THEMES

POLICE SUICIDE: ACUITY OF INFLUENCE
CODING SHEET: THEMES

Q 1.   What type(s) of difficult situations have you or
        another police officer have you come across in your
        law enforcement career that would lead you to
        consider suicide as a choice?

POLICE OFFICERS	THEMES
P1	NONE
P2	NONE
P3	NEVER CONSIDERED IT
P4	NONE
P5	NEVER CONSIDERED IT
P6	NEVER CONSIDERED IT
P7	NONE
P8	INTERNAL AFFAIRS INVESTIGATION
P9	NEVER CONSIDERED IT
P10	NONE
P11	NEVER CONSIDERED IT
P12	STRESSFUL EVENTS
P13	ENVIRONMENTAL FACTORS
P14	SURROUNDED BY SUICIDAL EVENTS
P15	NEVER CONSIDERED IT

POLICE SUICIDE: ACUITY OF INFLUENCE
CODING SHEET: THEMES

Q 2. **In retrospect to your experience with your present law enforcement organization, what type of in-service educational program did you undertake concerning the topic of suicide?**

POLICE OFFICERS	THEMES
P1	ESTABLISHINGING A TRAINING PROGRAM
P2	DON'T RECALL EVER COVER IN ACADEMY
P3	NEVER MENTIONED
P4	ZERO
P5	NO TRAINING
P6	NEVER AT ALL
P7	NONE
P8	TRAINING COURSE DEPARTMENT-WIDE
P9	NONE
P10	NONE
P11	NONE
P12	NONE
P13	NONE
P14	PLACE DOESN'T CARE ABOUT FAMILY MAN
P15	PREVENTIVE TRAINING

POLICE SUICIDE: ACUITY OF INFLUENCE
CODING SHEET: THEMES

Q 3.   Thinking back on the training you received with your present agency, what could have been done to improve and enhance the efficacy of the suicide education (if any)?

POLICE OFFICERS	THEMES
P1	THEY DON'T SHOW ANYTING
P2	YOU HAVE TO OFFER THIS TRAINING
P3	I DON'T THINK IT WOULD MAKE A DIFF
P4	COMMUNICATIONS, OUTREACH PROGRAM
P5	EAP PROGRAM
P6	OPEN FORUM/DEPT FROWNS ON IT
P7	DON'T KNOW ANYTHING ABOUT IT
P8	TRAINING (BEGIN AND END OF CAREER)
P9	CLASS/HOW TO GET THERAY
P10	GOOD IF IT EXISTED
P11	PROVIDED (NO DETAILS)
P12	ASIDE FROM WORKING WITH PEOPLE
P13	HUMAN DIVERSITY/NEVER ADDRESSED
P14	THEY DON'T DO ANYTHING
P15	WE DON'T GET THAT

POLICE SUICIDE: ACUITY OF INFLUENCE
CODING SHEET: THEMES

Q 4. Considering your experience with the agency you are employed with, in what ways does your police organization demonstrate concern about your welfare and on the issue of suicide?

POLICE OFFICERS	THEMES
P1	THEY DON'T SHOW ANYTHING
P2	NO OUTWARD CONCERNS
P3	THEY CAN CARE LESS
P4	THEY DON'T SHOW ANYTHING
P5	EAP PROGRAM
P6	NONE/NOBODY CARES/IMPERSONAL/NUM
P7	THEY DON'T CARE
P8	IT'S NEVR ABOUT THE GUYS HERE
P9	NONE AT ALL
P10	NEVER HEARD ANYTHING ABOUT IT
P11	EAP PROGRAM
P12	NO CAMARADERIE/DON'T CARE/NO CONFID
P13	THEY DON'T/DISPOSABLE
P14	EAP PROGRAM
P15	OUT OF CONTROL/EVERYBODY HURT HERE

POLICE SUICIDE: ACUITY OF INFLUENCE
CODING SHEET: THEMES

Q 5.	**What efforts do your peers do to diminish the strains that depression often exert on fellow officers that may consider suicide as an option?**

P1	I'VE NEVER HEARD OF ANYTHING
P2	I'VE NEVER HEARD OF ANYTHING
P3	SUPPORT/WE TALK/MY CREW
P4	THERE IS NO HELP
P5	I'VE NEVER HEARD OF ANYTHING
P6	NOT DISCUSSED/PANDORA'S BOX
P7	NOTHING
P8	RARELY ANY KIND OF ACTION IS TAKEN
P9	NOTHING
P10	I'VE NEVER HEARD OF ANYTHING
P11	DON'T KNOW OF ANYTHING
P12	VET SQUAD/PARK/CIGARS/DAILY/DEBRIEF
P13	TODAY, NOBODY HAS PEERS THAT TALK
P14	WE ALL TRY
P15	NOTHING IN PLACE/SIGNS IGNORED

POLICE SUICIDE: ACUITY OF INFLUENCE
CODING SHEET: THEMES

Q 6.   How do you view the police culture encumbering an officer's from ability to look for help on the subject of suicide?

POLICE OFFICERS	THEMES
P1	CULTURE/MACHO CULTURE
P2	CULTURE/SUPERMAN/MUST BE STRONGER
P3	YOU DON'T KNOW ABOUT IT/HOTLINE
P4	I DON'T SEE ANYTHING/IGNORING PROBLEM
P5	CULTURE/MENTAL ILLNESS LABELED CRAZY
P6	SEE OURSLEVES/NOTHING CAN AFFECT US
P7	NOTHING, THEY DO NOTHING
P8	MACHO ENVIRONMENT/SEEKING HELP/FROWNED
P9	DON'T KNOW WHAT HAPPENS IN CLOSED ROOM/FEAR
P10	NOT APPLICABLE
P11	SHOW OF WEAKNESS
P12	SWEPT UNDER CARPET
P13	INVISABLE
P14	REVEAL PROBLEM BEFORE PROMOTION/RISK/VULNER
P15	NO RESPONSE

POLICE SUICIDE: ACUITY OF INFLUENCE
CODING SHEET: THEMES

Q 7.   In retrospect to your experiences with your present law enforcement organization, what types of training programs have you had that would have addressed the issue of suicidal thoughts?

POLICE OFFICERS	THEMES
P1	NONE
P2	JUST SERVICES AVAILABLE/COUNSELING/WATEVER
P3	NONE
P4	NONE
P5	NONE
P6	NONE/WOULD BE WORTHWHILE
P7	NONE
P8	FEW COMMANDER CLASSES/BRIEFLY TOUCHED
P9	NONE
P10	NONE
P11	STRESS MANAGEMENT CLASS
P12	NONE
P13	NONE
P14	NONE
P15	NONE

POLICE SUICIDE: ACUITY OF INFLUENCE
CODING SHEET: THEMES

Q 8.   How do police supervisors and command staff speak to the issue of
police officer suicide in your law enforcement organization?

POLICE OFFICERS	THEMES
P1	ADRESS IT/NEVER ADDRESSED/DEPRESSION/FINAN
P2	BRIEF COUNSELING MAYBE/I DON'T THINK THEY DO
P3	THEY DON'T WANT TO KNOW ABOUT IT/LIABILITY
P4	NONE
P5	I'VE NEVER HEARD IT ADDRESSED
P6	THEY DON'T/THEY HOPE IT DOESN'T HAPPEN
P7	THEY DON'T
P8	I'VE NEVER HEARD IT ADDRESSED
P9	THEY DON'T
P10	NEVER HAPPENED
P11	SOMETHING PEOPLE DON'T TALK ABOUT
P12	NONE
P13	NONE/NOBODY EVEN TALKS ABOUT IT
P14	NO RESPONSE
P15	NO RESPONSE

POLICE SUICIDE: ACUITY OF INFLUENCE
CODING SHEET: THEMES

Q 9.   How can police supervisors and command staff ward off the risk of suicide as an option for your fellow officers?

POLICE OFFICERS	THEMES
P1	ADDRESS IT
P2	HAVE INFORMAL MEETING/SHOW CONCERN
P3	IT'S A JOB/HUMAN FACTOR/THEY DON'T CARE/US
P4	PROGRAMS/TALK ABOUT IT/MECHANISM/NOT CARING
P5	DISTRUCT/CINFIDENTIALITY/RESOURSE OUTSIDE
P6	KEEN EYE TO WATCH/PROCEDURES/FOLLOW-UP
P7	TRAINING CLASSES/PSYCHOLOGIST
P8	COUNSELING/ANGER MANGEMENT COURSE
P9	SUPERVISOR MORE IN TUNE/DON'T CARE ABOUT YOU
P10	OFFER A PROGRAM/NOT HERE
P11	PROVIDE TRAINING/SUICIDE PREVENTION/EAP
P12	MAKE SUPERVISORS AWARE
P13	SPENCER RULE/DON'T WANT TO SEE
P14	THEY US ETHE WORD GOD/PONTIFICATE/HOMELESS
P15	NO RESPONSE

APPENDIX F: INDIVIDUAL INTERVIEW TRANSCRIPTS

July 2013
Jeffersonian Transcription Notation
Standard Rules for Transcription
(Atkinson and Heritage, 1984)

Capitalization

I followed the standard written capitalization patterns where applicable, and capitalize words at the beginning of a sentence, with proper names.

Spelling

Whenever possible, I tried to use correct spelling (what is customarily referred to as orthography) and or word segmentation, except where explicitly specified otherwise; whenever in doubt about the spelling of a word or name, I typically accepted in these cases reviewed acceptable reference material.

Contractions

Whenever a contraction was used, I always made sure to insert whenever it was actually said by the officer. I tried always to transcribe exactly what the officer said, not what I expected to hear. If the officer used a contraction, the word was transcribed as contracted: they're, won't, isn't, don't and so on. If the officer used a complete form of the word, I transcribed exactly what I heard (i.e., they are, is not, etc.).

I made use of common contractions. When I heard them, I used the nonstandard forms gonna, wanna, gotta, shoulda, woulda, coulda instead of standard orthography, especially if this is how an officer normally pronounces the words in question. I also made sure to avoid the common mistakes of transposing possessive it's for the contraction it's (it is); possessive you're for the contraction you're (you are); and their (possessive), they're (they are) and there.

Numbers

All numerals were written out as complete words. Hyphenation was used for numbers between twenty-one and ninety-nine only (i.e., twenty-two, nineteen ninety-five, seven thousand two hundred seventy-five or nineteen oh nine, etc.).

Hyphenated Words and Compounds

I used hyphens in compounds where they were required (i.e., full-off, not full off protests). In cases where there was a choice between writing a compound word as one word, a hyphenated word, or as two words with spaces in between, I opted for one of the latter two versions (i.e., house-builder, house builder not housebuilder)

Abbreviations

When at all possible, I tried to avoid using abbreviations. The words spoken were transcribed exactly as spoken by the officers. The exception would be made whenever the abbreviation were used as part of a personal title, in such cases; they remain as abbreviations, as in standard writing (i.e., Maj. Santiago, Ofc. Tom McEvoy, etc.). However, when they were used in any other contexts, I would write them out in full.

Acronyms and Spoken Letters

Acronyms that are normally written as a single word but pronounced as a sequence of individual letters were written in all caps, with each individual letter surrounded by spaces (i.e., EAP, DROP, etc.). Similarly, any instances where individual letters are pronounced as such, were written in caps:

Punctuation

I used standard punctuation for ease of transcription and reading comprehension. Punctuation was written as it normally appears in standard writing, with no additional spaces around the punctuation marks. Acceptable punctuation is limited to periods, exclamation marks and question marks at the end of a sentence, and commas within a sentence. Exclamation marks are used for especially emphatic speech.

Quotation Marks

Quotation marks were used to indicate direct speech or thoughts within a specific narrative and was used consistently for that purpose only.

Introduction

Disfluent speech is particularly difficult to transcribe. The officers at times repeated themselves, utter partial words, restart phrases or sentences, and use numerous hesitation sounds. I tried to take particular care in sections where disfluent speech was used to transcribe exactly what is spoken, including all of the partial words, repetitions and filled pauses used by the speaker.

Filled Pauses and Hesitation Sounds

Filled pauses are non-lexemes (non-words) that the officers interviewed often employed to indicate hesitation and or to maintain control of a conversation while thinking of what to say next. There was a limited set of filled pauses that each officer employed in their speech patterns.

Filled Pauses

The spelling of filled pauses was restricted (i.e., ah, eh, er, uh, and um).

Partial Words

When an officer broke off in the middle of the word, I tried, as much as I could, to transcribe as much of the word as can be made out. A single dash without preceding space - was used to indicate a point at which word were broken off. If I was able to make a reasonable guess at which word were intended by the officers, I included the full form of the word immediately after the truncated form, preceded by a plus sign + (without separating spaces) when applicable.

Restarts

Restarts are indicated with double dash – surrounded by spaces. This is often commonly used in cases where an interviewee stops abruptly, cutting themselves off before continuing with or rephrasing the utterance (using words like "uh").

Mispronounced or Non-standard Words

An asterisk * was used for mispronounced words (not regional or non-standard dialect pronunciation in format), or for words that are made up on the spot by an officer or are idiosyncratic to the law enforcement profession's usage. I tried using the standard spelling and did not try to represent the pronunciation.

Unclear or Unintelligible Speech

Sometimes an audio file contained a section of speech that was difficult or impossible for me to understand. In these cases, I used double parentheses (( )) to mark the region of difficulty.

If it was possible for me to make a guess about an officer's words, I attempted to transcribe what I think I heard and surround the stretch of uncertain transcription with double parentheses

Interjections

The following standardized spellings were used to transcribe interjections. Interjections do not require any special symbol (i.e., Duh, eee, ew, ha, hee, huh, huh-uh (neg.), hm, yeah, etc.).

Other Transcription Symbols

In addition to the transcription conventions outlined, the following symbols were used for the transcription of other kinds of noises made by either the main speaker or one of the other officers in the interviews:

    {BR}   breath (The speaker takes an audible breath.)
    {CG}   cough(The speaker coughs, or clears his/her throat.)
    {LS}   lip smack (The speaker smacks his/her lips.)
    {LG}   laughter (The speaker laughs.)
    {NS}   noise(Loud background noise)

Formal Methods and Style Coding

If a recording contains a section on formal methods (i.e. a part of the interview where an officer may have been explicitly asked to read out texts or word lists, or to make judgments about language use), the appropriate two-letter style codes would have be indicated on a separate style tier.

Code   Formal Method

The officer (if utilized and applicable) is asked to read aloud pairs of words and is asked whether they differ in pronunciation.(i.e., SD -Semantic differential, RP - Reading passage, WL - Word list, MP - Minimal pairs:

Some General Considerations

I made no attempt to correct non-standard grammatical features; e.g." I seen him" for "I saw him." The same went for words that were used in a non-standard way, I transcribed what was spoken, not what I expected to hear.

Transcript: Individual Interview
Control Number: 2013-01-(P1)
Research: Police Suicide: Acuity of Influence
By: Michael J. Alicea, MS, MSW

DEMOGRAPHICS
Gender: Male
Race and or Ethnicity: White
Age: 46-55
Current Marital Status: Married
Education - Highest Degree Held: High School
Employment: Coral Gables Police Department, State of Florida
Type of Law Enforcement Agency: Municipal Agency
Title: Police Officer
Length of Service: 25 years or more

I: *What type(s) of difficult situations have you or another police officer have you come across in your law enforcement career that would lead you to consider suicide as a choice?*
P1: None

I: *In retrospect to your experience with your present law enforcement organization, what type of in-service educational program did you undertake concerning the topic of suicide?*
P1: None

I: *Thinking back on the training you received with your present agency, what could have been done to improve and enhance the efficacy of the suicide education (if any)?*
P1: To establish a training program, a regular training program, I don't think we have one, I've never seen an establish program that deals with that. I know they have one in the military, because of all the military suicides they have. It's a lot of 'fuckin'' people. More than people that gets killed on the battlefield. As far as I know, they had to establish something before they can improve upon, I would think.

I: *Considering your experience with the agency you are employed with, in what ways does your police organization demonstrate concern about your welfare and on the issue of suicide?*
P1: Our administration, like in our Chief? Our well being, I don't think they show anything, on either issue, I don't think they even address the other issue.

I: *What efforts do your peers do to diminish the strains that depression often exert on fellow officers that may consider suicide as an option?*
P1: I don't think I've ever dealt with anybody that knows if someone is considering suicide as an option, maybe you have, because people will come and talk to you, because of your profession, I've never heard of, I don't know of any.

I: *How do you view the police culture encumbering an officer's from ability to look for help on the subject of suicide?*
P1: Because it is the culture, that macho culture, you know, you're considered to be a "pussy" or a weak individual if you're considering suicide, rather than admit to depression, you closet it.

I: *In retrospect to your experiences with your present law enforcement organization, what types of training programs have you had that would have addressed the issue of suicidal thoughts?*
P1: None. Well, I've only seen it once within this particular department and they ignored it that was with Tommy Mac. They just kind of brushed it aside. They didn't really give a "shit" about it. At least not what I saw.

I: *How can police supervisors and command staff ward off the risk of suicide as an option for your fellow officers?*
P1: Address it to begin with. They need to address it before they can improve or assist on anything until they'll willing to address the issue. Tommy Mac, they never addressed the issue, and even after he did it (referring to suicide) The Major of Uniform Patrol had lunch an hour later while the guy was sitting there dead in the back of the station, this person was the Patrol Division Major. That's how much she (Major) gave a "shit." I didn't know the guy, the guy that I actually trained with in Metro, I worked with, he actually committed suicide, but he had a lot of family issues. I think everything with him was with his family. His wife was leaving him, you know his kids, and he couldn't deal with that. I don't think it was so much the job, but who knows what's in somebody's mind when they do that, you're never going to find out, they don't leave any information. I didn't tell you anything you didn't already know. I was trying to think of something humorous, but I can't. No, I don't think that "shit" has ever been addressed here, or in any police department that I've ever been in. I've never heard of it ever being addressed. It happens, depression, I think depression "fuckin" rampant in this job. Between personal issues, the shit they (police officers) sees, the financial problems that everyone has, I think the "fuckin" depression is easily as rampant here if not more so in the civilian population.

Transcript: Individual Interview
Control Number: 2013-02-(P2)
Research: Police Suicide: Acuity of Influence
By: Michael J. Alicea, MS, MSW

DEMOGRAPHICS
Gender: Male
Race and or Ethnicity: Hispanic
Age: 46-55
Current Marital Status: Married
Education - Highest Degree Held: AA
Employment: Coral Gables Police Department, State of Florida
Type of Law Enforcement Agency: Municipal Agency
Title: Police Officer
Length of Service: 20 years or more

I: *What type(s) of difficult situations have you or another police officer have you come across in your law enforcement career that would lead you to consider suicide as a choice?*
P2: None.

I: *In retrospect to your experience with your present law enforcement organization, what type of in-service educational program did you undertake concerning the topic of suicide?*
P2: Training, Umm, I don't recall that they ever covered that in the Academy, certainly nothing since the Academy. We may have touched it.

I: *Thinking back on the training you received with your present agency, what could have been done to improve and enhance the efficacy of the suicide education (if any)?*
P2: Well, first of all, you have to offer this training; it should be something on a voluntary basis. I think it should at least be offered.

I: *Considering your experience with the agency you are employed with, in what ways does your police organization demonstrate concern about your welfare and on the issue of suicide?*
P2: I don't, I don't see any kind of outward concerns, physical or with mental health, to be honest with you. They just want us to come and do our job (laugh). They don't care what's going on with our personal life. I mean they use that service that they provide, yes, EAP (Employee Assistance Program), they mentioned that.

I: *What efforts do your peers do to diminish the strains that depression often exert on fellow officers that may consider suicide as an option?*
P2: I mean, I haven't seen any obvious attempts to by anybody to, but then again that is something that I don't project that I guess I'm suicidal, I would like to think that, just talking with people, with each other would help somebody in that situation. I don't know really. It happens.

I: *How do you view the police culture encumbering an officer's from ability to look for help on the subject of suicide?*
P2: Umm, the culture you know, Superman, you know, kinda ideology, stereotypes, that we have to be stronger than other people. So that would lead to, you know, to someone coming out and express what they were feeling, concerning suicidal tendencies, especially the fact that we carry weapons.

I: *In retrospect to your experiences with your present law enforcement organization, what types of training programs have you had that would have addressed the issue of suicidal thoughts?*
P2: Didn't you asked that, just the services, counseling, whatever.

I: *How do police supervisors and command staff speak to the issue of police officer suicide in your law enforcement organization?*
P2: Umm, I don't think they do. They don't address it. I wasn't here during the last one, but, I don't know, I don't know if it was addressed at all. Brief counseling maybe?

I: *How can police supervisors and command staff ward off the risk of suicide as an option for your fellow officers?*
P2: How could they assist, Umm, (long pause), Umm, an indication I think would be, you know, have an informal meeting with people, everyone, you know, for example: How's your family? Show more concern I guess.

Transcript: Individual Interview
Control Number: 2013-03-(P3)
Research: Police Suicide: Acuity of Influence
By: Michael J. Alicea, MS, MSW

DEMOGRAPHICS
Gender: Male
Race and or Ethnicity: Hispanic
Age: 36-45
Current Marital Status: Married
Education - Highest Degree Held: High School
Employment: Coral Gables Police Department, State of Florida
Type of Law Enforcement Agency: Municipal Agency
Title: Police Officer
Length of Service: 15 years or more

I: *What type(s) of difficult situations have you or another police officer have you come across in your law enforcement career that would lead you to consider suicide as a choice?*
P3: Never. I've never considered suicide ever. Period. Even on my "baddist" days have I ever considered suicide.

I: *In retrospect to your experience with your present law enforcement organization, what type of in-service educational program did you undertake concerning the topic of suicide?*
P3: It's never been mentioned at all. The first I've ever heard of a question regarding suicide. {LG}

I: *Thinking back on the training you received with your present agency, what could have been done to improve and enhance the efficacy of the suicide education (if any)?*
P3: I'm sorry (repeat the question)? I don't think it would make a difference usually the question is suicide or suicide attempt? Yeah, anything is good to have a fundamental, Ahh, is that what Crisis Intervention Training (CIT) is? Oh I see. I guess it would help to have some type of understanding, how people are thinking what they're thinking. I know one good real good friend of mine who shot himself, I forgot his last name, it was a steroid issue. They were going to have to amputate his arm; he shot himself with a shotgun. Over, five or six years ago, in fact, it may have been more than five or six years.

I: *Considering your experience with the agency you are employed with, in what ways does your police organization demonstrate concern about your welfare and on the issue of suicide?*

P3: They can care less I believe. It's not even a topic. It's not even talked about.

I: *What efforts do your peers do to diminish the strains that depression often exert on fellow officers that may consider suicide as an option?*

P3: Well, the people I work with, if I'm depressed or sad or having a bad day, they'll come and talk to me, or they'll offer "a take it easy" they're caring. I think they become more friends at that point. I could see my crew, the people I work with, and only them, for me and support me for anything that I may need or a place to stay, or money or anything I think I might need. But that's just my peers. I mean I don't expect that from the midnight people, or expect that from the morning crew, because I really don't have a relationship with them. We say hi and bye to each other.

I: *How do you view the police culture encumbering an officer's from ability to look for help on the subject of suicide?*

P3: Well there is a hotline, right, no one knows about it, I just don't know how to get to it, or, if you don't know about it, how to seek it, and Ahh, we have one, in the five or six years that I've been here, we've only had one guy come once, and let us know about it. But that is something that should be reminded to us constantly, like everything else. It should be reinforced, period, at least once or twice a year at least in the Officer Survival Training Program. Have some guy come out and just remind us that it's there. These online courses take away the community contact. It's crazy. That's crazy.

I: *In retrospect to your experiences with your present law enforcement organization, what types of training programs have you had that would have addressed the issue of suicidal thoughts?*

P3: None. I don't know why, all we have is our personal life experiences and just common sense I would think to some extent. All we have is each other.

I: *How do police supervisors and command staff speak to the issue of police officer suicide in your law enforcement organization?*

P3: I don't know, and honestly I don't think they want to know about it because then there is possibly a liability, it's the last thing anyone wants to hear. I don't know you that well, but I think we have a bond from our past, I mean your much older than me, or experience, you've been there longer, and of a different era, it's nice that we have that understanding, you know. The other people (Officers) will never understand.

I: *How can police supervisors and command staff ward off the risk of suicide as an option for your fellow officers?*

P3: Well, Number one, don't forget we're we started, I mean, this is just a job, it's basically a job. Forget about the departmental orders, or administrative policies, what about the human factor, you know, we all make mistakes? They (administrators) want to live by the book, they just want to burn you and make your life miserable, what about us, taking care of us. But as shifts go on, schedule changes we all have families, you know, yet we don't get the credit or appreciation. I've yet to see all those "fuckin" officers and "bullshit" who receive officer of the mouth commendations that means nothing, there's nothing better than a pat on the back saying hey "thank you." They don't get that. I've seen names of offices on the walls, who looks at that? Nobody, just the POD (Police Operations Desk) officer. That's it! There's nothing more satisfying than a pat on the back or barbecue with your crew, being one-on-one, those awards mean nothing to me that's why I have no ambition or inhibitions to move up. It's like parents and children you know, I'm your father but your friend first. Same thing here, we should, shouldn't have to, say hey Sarge, why can I call you by your first name, this isn't the "freakin" military. You know, give me a break, you know, this place is so paranoid. One thing I have that police work has done to me, I've lost all my emotional, and I don't feel sensitive to my emotions anymore. If someone gets hit by a car, I can care less. I've lost all my emotions because, because they don't care about us. I hear the calls go out, I hear the dispatcher get excited, the other guys get excited because they are responding, and I'm like, whatever, en route, I can care less. With family, when my father passed away, I cried, you know, I guess I'm in touch with my family, my emotions when it comes to my family. But if someone is in an accident, I can care less. You want a report; it bothers me to see everybody else so involved, why do they care so much? I guess this is their "bread and butter", that is something else that someone else can do. It's crazy. I see, I've become a sourpuss, dude, policing has changed, and you're out there doing stupid things, and this is Coral Gables, it's really hard to do something stupid but when it's done; I've had 15 or 20 of my friends (Officers) that have been arrested, or fired. You know, my academy class, there is probably just seven of us left. And, I don't want to be a statistic, you know. And I guess, I answer my calls, don't get me wrong, it bothers me sometimes, until you walk in my shoes, or you have lost someone. When Officer (referring to an officer that was arrested), was arrested for doing his job, you know, whether you did it right or wrong, you did your job. And it's easy to criticize someone, and play "Monday Morning Quarterback", Oh, I should've done this I should've done that, until your there. I have a friend of mine, (referring to an officer that is doing time in the State Penitentiary), he's doing four years in jail, he was a Sergeant at CST (Specialized Task Force) in Miami, and you know they did some "dirty work," I guess. But you know, that's just part of life, you want numbers, then justify to play, and "bro," four years of his life for nothing, he's not getting anything for that. Nothing, he was just doing his job. This "bull-shit" with the SIT (Special Investigative Team – Undercover Unit) team, I told, listen, I don't want to go and lose my days off for something in vain. You know, I expect accountability, from getting "fucked" with these days off, these guys better not be scamming, I choose not to be in that unit, but they choose to. But if I might get burned by this unit, I expect numbers, I want them or expect them to not be "fuckin off", you know how you know how it is, too much liberty, they'll take advantage of it. Then they go six or eight hours doing nothing because, unless its traffic oriented, what the "fuck" are they going to do out there? What are they going to do? What are they going to do here, traffic, unless the call goes out? They are going to "fuck" with the wrong "motherfucker"; an educated "motherfucker." It's different from working in Miami in Wynwood and Allapattah (High crime neighborhoods in Miami) when what you find there is pieces of "shit." People here are educated (Spanish). What are they going to do? {LG}

Transcript: Individual Interview
Control Number: 2013-04-(P4)
Research: Police Suicide: Acuity of Influence
By: Michael J. Alicea, MS, MSW

DEMOGRAPHICS
Gender: Male
Race and or Ethnicity: White
Age: 36-45
Current Marital Status: Married
Education - Highest Degree Held: BA
Employment: Coral Gables Police Department, State of Florida
Type of Law Enforcement Agency: Municipal Agency
Title: Police Officer
Length of Service: 15 years or more

I: *What type(s) of difficult situations have you or another police officer have you come across in your law enforcement career that would lead you to consider suicide as a choice?*
P4: I haven't gone into anything here. I've been all right.

I: *In retrospect to your experience with your present law enforcement organization, what type of in-service educational program did you undertake concerning the topic of suicide?*
P4: No, zero.

I: *Thinking back on the training you received with your present agency, what could have been done to improve and enhance the efficacy of the suicide education (if any)?*
P4: What could have been improved? Yes, I remember McEvoy the Police Officer that committed suicide). No communications. No outreach. No one reached out to him.

I: *Considering your experience with the agency you are employed with, in what ways does your police organization demonstrate concern about your welfare and on the issue of suicide?*
P4: They don't show anything.

I: *What efforts do your peers do to diminish the strains that depression often exert on fellow officers that may consider suicide as an option?*
P4: There is no help.

I: *How do you view the police culture encumbering an officer's from ability to look for help on the subject of suicide?*
P4: I don't see anything. It's more of ignoring the problem; that you should "suck it up."

I: *In retrospect to your experiences with your present law enforcement organization, what types of training programs have you had that would have addressed the issue of suicidal thoughts?*
P4: None.

I: *How do police supervisors and command staff speak to the issue of police officer suicide in your law enforcement organization?*
P4: There's none.

I: *How can police supervisors and command staff ward off the risk of suicide as an option for your fellow officers?*
P4: Programs, talk about it. We have incidents like what happened to McEvoy, why weren't there any failsafe mechanisms to help him. If you think about it, his children, his stress with his ex-wife, going to court, and a shift that didn't work for him, taking care of is children, reference, had to make an appeal to accommodate taking his kids to school, after work, and he couldn't work shift hours given to help pick-up his children, stress on that. Not caring. Ignoring his needs, and coming to the station, and doing the suicide just to make a point; they still don't talk about it. They're still the same way they, haven't changed. But, in police work as in other departments, they have suicide prevention, we don't, why not? I guess because we don't have too many suicides like the other departments do. Things could get worse.

Control Number: 2013-05-(P5)
Research: Police Suicide: Acuity of Influence
By: Michael J. Alicea, MS, MSW

DEMOGRAPHICS
Gender: Male
Race and or Ethnicity: Black
Age: 36-45
Current Marital Status: Divorced
Education - Highest Degree Held: AA
Employment: Coral Gables Police Department, State of Florida
Type of Law Enforcement Agency: Municipal Agency
Title: Police Officer
Length of Service: 15 years or more

I: *What type(s) of difficult situations have you or another police officer have you come across in your law enforcement career that would lead you to consider suicide as a choice?*
P5: That could have? That could have, me personally? I could never have considered it.

I: *In retrospect to your experience with your present law enforcement organization, what type of in-service educational program did you undertake concerning the topic of suicide?*
P5: No training but, I'm aware of programs like EAP.

I: *Thinking back on the training you received with your present agency, what could have been done to improve and enhance the efficacy of the suicide education (if any)?*
P5: Umm, could you repeat that one more time? Ummm, it wasn't training, it was, you know, Umm, it was just explained about the availability of, EAP program.

I: *Considering your experience with the agency you are employed with, in what ways does your police organization demonstrate concern about your welfare and on the issue of suicide?*
P5: Umm, by providing you Employee Assistance Program (EAP) and anything else.

I: *What efforts do your peers do to diminish the strains that depression often exert on fellow officers that may consider suicide as an option?*
P5: I'm not aware of any.

I: *How do you view the police culture encumbering an officer's from ability to look for help on the subject of suicide?*

P5: Umm, Umm, {BR}, I think there is Umm, and overall culture, Umm, and law enforcement, that ah, you know Ahh, that Ahh, how do I want to put this, (pause),Umm, you know, that anyone with mental illness is just labeled crazy. Umm, the term 43 (Police code/signal for someone who is a 'Baker Act" and or mentally challenged), is used loosely, and that Umm, {BR} always then not us.

I: *In retrospect to your experiences with your present law enforcement organization, what types of training programs have you had that would have addressed the issue of suicidal thoughts?*

P5: {BR} None.

I: *How do police supervisors and command staff speak to the issue of police officer suicide in your law enforcement organization?*

P5: I've never heard it addressed.

I: *How can police supervisors and command staff ward off the risk of suicide as an option for your fellow officers?*

P5: Umm, Umm, {BR} what can they do? {BR}, I think, Umm, you know, we tend to not, Umm, what was explained to us as confidentiality. You know and, it's been my experience with my peers and everything, Umm, {BR} that confidential is not necessarily confidential. You know and, where Umm, {BR} you know there's a lot of distrust, you know that whatever you tell someone hopefully isn't going to come back and bite you one day. You know, so I think that Umm, {BR} if there were a resource maybe, outside of the police department, Umm, {BR} and you know I understand EAP is supposed to be outside of the police department, but yeah, Umm, you know not necessarily the police department, you know Umm, the city government that Umm, whatever you confide in someone, you know, it's going to be confidential, you know that you won't see again. So, Umm, you know, I don't know, that Umm, {BR} I would ever, Umm. Umm, I would completely trust agencies or government, Umm, administration Umm, {BR} you know resources, you know

Transcript: Individual Interview
Control Number: 2013-06-(P6)
Research: Police Suicide: Acuity of Influence
By: Michael J. Alicea, MS, MSW

DEMOGRAPHICS
Gender: Male
Race and or Ethnicity: Hispanic
Age: 36-45
Current Marital Status: Married
Education - Highest Degree Held: AA
Employment: Coral Gables Police Department, State of Florida
Type of Law Enforcement Agency: Municipal Agency
Title: Police Officer
Length of Service: 20 years or more

I: *What type(s) of difficult situations have you or another police officer have you come across in your law enforcement career that would lead you to consider suicide as a choice?*

P6: I've never considered suicide. I've seen some horrific things, but it's never crossed my mind.

I: *In retrospect to your experience with your present law enforcement organization, what type of in-service educational program did you undertake concerning the topic of suicide?*

P6: Never at all. None that I have ever have taken, Umm, either at the beginning of my career, or throughout. They have offered, actually, a program available with a psychologists, Umm, either on-call, I know they have a program for that. I think they came out with some type of pamphlet if I'm not mistaken, maybe a year or a year and a half ago. And, actually I haven't seen it from my boss for a while. Any issues, suicides, I don't know, alcohol, drugs or anything like that.

I: *Thinking back on the training you received with your present agency, what could have been done to improve and enhance the efficacy of the suicide education (if any)?*

P6: I think discussing it would be a good idea. Having an open forum where you can tie it into any class you want to tie it where you can have a couple hours of open discussion. As people talk about it. It's a start. I think the department frowns upon it. I personally don't like to go to police funerals, I went to one once, and I swore I would never go to one again. I don't know if it's denial or where it would fall unto, but, Umm, I don't know what it would fall equivalent to. I'd probably would still not talk about it.

I: *Considering your experience with the agency you are employed with, in what ways does your police organization demonstrate concern about your welfare and on the issue of suicide?*

P6: None at all. I mean I recently got bit by one of our dogs in training, and I had hand surgery, nobody found out. Nobody bothered to call. It was just a simple dog bite, I had to go through surgery, I was out for a couple months, and nobody called me. Taking it a step even higher than that, and for suicide, I don't think nobody really cares. I think it's gotten more impersonal, the department that is. I think years ago it was a little bit more tight, but, Umm, oh well. I think we've become a number. That was part of the reason why I was attracted to this department; it was big enough and small enough where everyone knew each other. I think we have gotten so far away from that, everyone has become a number here, and I think, Umm, I think it is across the country, not just here. I think it's just something that is happening across the country. I couldn't talk from experience, but I think it's pretty pervasive.

I: *What efforts do your peers do to diminish the strains that depression often exert on fellow officers that may consider suicide as an option?*

P6: I think it's something that doesn't get discussed. I think that when guys get depressed they get isolated, we isolate them, just talking about that, that officer that we were just talking about, oh yeah, he has lost a lot of weight. We've become so impersonal and I think it has to start somewhere from a leadership role to make things more personal. To reach out. We tend to get away from people we are afraid of. It's sort of like the fear of opening up a "Pandora's Box" for ourselves. Along with that, we're scared that he may rub off on us. It might open up some wound for us, and say wait a minute; he's no better than I am. Maybe something to look at.

I: *How do you view the police culture encumbering an officer's from ability to look for help on the subject of suicide?*

P6: I think people reach out so much for help that I think that we see ourselves as if nothing can affect us. So, I think if we were to reach out, I think it would make us incompetent to do the job. Mentally I think we would think now I am incompetent to do the job. I guess here I am helping this person out, but eight hours ago, I was sitting in a couch. So I think that's why, fear of acknowledging that we are human, and fear that maybe we can't do our job. If we are expressing our issues, whatever issues we have, with a therapists, I think 10 hours later we come here to do our job how am I going to be helping out; it's like an alcoholic stopping a person for DUI. It makes no sense what so ever. Why am I even doing it? So, I think that maybe one of the issues.

I: *In retrospect to your experiences with your present law enforcement organization, what types of training programs have you had that would have addressed the issue of suicidal thoughts?*

P6: None. I can't remember any. I think it would be worthwhile to pursue. Our CIT (Crisis Intervention Training) training may have had a small part or component about suicide, but it must have been a small part, I don't remember. It was nothing about us.

I: *How do police supervisors and command staff speak to the issue of police officer suicide in your law enforcement organization?*

P6: I think they don't. I think is something that they hope it doesn't happen, there is no preventive maintenance at all, I mean none at all. None. We're definitely not proactive, we're definitely reactive. If there are reactive measures, I don't know what those reaction measures are. I'm sure they have measures in place so that if something should happen, to get that call, to a family member of ours, but I am not in a position to know. It would be a great idea to know, but it will never happen. I could never see myself going into my SOP (Standard Operating Procedures) manual and seeing that, I just don't see it. Again, going back to the thing about suicide, nobody wants to discuss it.

I: *How can police supervisors and command staff ward off the risk of suicide as an option for your fellow officers?*

P6: I don't know, the front line supervisor should have enough of a keen eye to watch people, to see that they've lost some weight, I mean you can see it, we've seen them here. I don't know if there is something in place, or position to start stepping in. I mean they have procedures when we get contacts (reference complaints from the public) from the public, steps, procedures, do they have that for people who are sick, I don't know. I don't know where we are with that. We should absolutely have that. This topic has never personally crossed my mind, I've seen it happen here in our department, it's funny because it affects the department for a couple of months, a couple of months afterwards, they act like it never happened. It just never happened. Nobody ever follows up with that case. Umm, you try to separate yourself from him, because of XYZ, it will never happen to me. Back in those days, I was in motors, I remember him (Police Officer that committed suicide), and he was always back there smoking, always, always. I would ask him how are you doing. I'm okay, I'm okay. I remember him out there always out there. But I don't think anyone ever reached out to him, whatever came out of that. I don't know whatever really happened. I think his reason was the department, I think he was angry, if he came all the way over here just for that, the main reason, for his suicide, whatever happened in the department, whatever issues he had with the department, I don't remember what they were. Umm, no doubt in my mind. Was there an injury, I don't know, was he taken off the road because of low energy, I don't know. I'm thinking right now, I know that it would never happen, we as police officers have so much stress, mostly from inside the department. Mostly, Umm, I think a great program would be a set number of questions and have somebody just sit down and see us as a police officer, have a therapist in here, to sit and talk with us and ask the question: What's bothering you, is there anything that is bothering you? And, talk about it. Sometimes we get so locked in hard thing and we get so blinded.

Transcript: Individual Interview
Control Number: 2013-07-(P7)
Research: Police Suicide: Acuity of Influence
By: Michael J. Alicea, MS, MSW

DEMOGRAPHICS
Gender: Male
Race and or Ethnicity: White
Age: 46-55
Current Marital Status: Divorced
Education - Highest Degree Held: AA
Employment: Coral Gables Police Department, State of Florida
Type of Law Enforcement Agency: Municipal Agency
Title: Police Officer
Length of Service: 25 years or more

I: *What type(s) of difficult situations have you or another police officer have you come across in your law enforcement career that would lead you to consider suicide as a choice?*
P7: None.

I: *In retrospect to your experience with your present law enforcement organization, what type of in-service educational program did you undertake concerning the topic of suicide?*
P7: None.

I: *Thinking back on the training you received with your present agency, what could have been done to improve and enhance the efficacy of the suicide education (if any)?*
P7: I don't know anything about it. Oh yeah, they could have created something. Yeah they could have seen him (Police Officer who committed suicide). They should have taken his gun from him, or put him on administrative leave, or send him to that guy (psychologist), or that guy would comes here and tells him what he should do, I guess not because of confidentiality. I mean I know that's all they do.

I: *Considering your experience with the agency you are employed with, in what ways does your police organization demonstrate concern about your welfare and on the issue of suicide?*
P7: They don't.

I: *What efforts do your peers do to diminish the strains that depression often exert on fellow officers that may consider suicide as an option?*
P7: Nothing.

I: *How do you view the police culture encumbering an officer's from ability to look for help on the subject of suicide?*
P7: Nothing, they do nothing.

I: *In retrospect to your experiences with your present law enforcement organization, what types of training programs have you had that would have addressed the issue of suicidal thoughts?*
P7: None.

I: *How do police supervisors and command staff speak to the issue of police officer suicide in your law enforcement organization?*
P7: They don't.

I: *How can police supervisors and command staff ward off the risk of suicide as an option for your fellow officers?*
P7: How can they assess? They train classes. They should take these training classes. Oh, no, well, well they should recommend, I want you guys to get this training, we need people to recognize the signs. Right now, I think if they think you're going to commit suicide. To move you here to go to this guy (psychologist), go ahead and see what's wrong, and that's it. Nobody really knows what to do. I wouldn't know what to do. I don't have the training. You need someone to train people, on what to do, and things to do, to help these people. Reasonable.

Transcript: Individual Interview
Control Number: 2013-08-(P8)
Research: Police Suicide: Acuity of Influence
By: Michael J. Alicea, MS, MSW

DEMOGRAPHICS
Gender: Male
Race and or Ethnicity: Other
Age: 36-45
Current Marital Status: Separated
Education - Highest Degree Held: BA
Employment: Coral Gables Police Department, State of Florida
Type of Law Enforcement Agency: Municipal Agency
Title: Police Lieutenant
Length of Service: 15 years or more

I: *What type(s) of difficult situations have you or another police officer have you come across in your law enforcement career that would lead you to consider suicide as a choice?*
P8: Ahh, Internal Affairs investigations.

I: *In retrospect to your experience with your present law enforcement organization, what type of in-service educational program did you undertake concerning the topic of suicide?*
P8: Ahh, well, one of the best emotional survival for police officers. Ahh, (referred to a commander in the Department overseeing Special Investigations Section). I volunteered for it many years ago and then in one of the annual training advisory meetings we had I recommended it to senior staff and it was actually implemented as a training course department-wide. It was one of those online things you had to go on, one of those on-line courses, but it's never about the guys here. It was too expensive, but it did have the whole course online. Everybody did it online. Ahh, one of the class I went to, one of the best class I went to, talks about the stages of your career and the environment that you work in and the emotional ups and downs as far as the cycle of daily police work.

I: *Thinking back on the training you received with your present agency, what could have been done to improve and enhance the efficacy of the suicide education (if any)?*
P8: Ahh, this training would be a great proceeded to suicide, to give you an overall picture of your emotional fluctuation as a police officer. So I think they should be some kind of training at least in your first five years as a police officer concerning suicide. At least in the beginning and towards the end.

I: *Considering your experience with the agency you are employed with, in what ways does your police organization demonstrate concern about your welfare and on the issue of suicide?*
P8: Currently, none.

I: *What efforts do your peers do to diminish the strains that depression often exert on fellow officers that may consider suicide as an option?*
P8: Very rarely any kind of action is taken.

I: *How do you view the police culture encumbering an officer's from ability to look for help on the subject of suicide?*
P8: Ahh, it is still very much a macho environment, so the mere fact that seeing a shrink or psychologist is probably still frown upon.

I: *In retrospect to your experiences with your present law enforcement organization, what types of training programs have you had that would have addressed the issue of suicidal thoughts?*
P8: After taking the class, I actually I had a few commander classes where we touch briefly on it but not very much in depth to the training program.

I: *How do police supervisors and command staff speak to the issue of police officer suicide in your law enforcement organization?*
P8: It really hasn't been addressed per se.

I: *How can police supervisors and command staff ward off the risk of suicide as an option for your fellow officers?*
P8: I think a big, step that they should make; I mean we recently had off-duty officers arrested, in the past year, more so than ever. And I don't know personally if those, offices where given any type of counseling. I don't think they were. I know one was mandated for an anger management course but that was after the fact, so I don't think they realize the impact it also has being arrested or about to be arrested and as a critical stage. So I think this should be something built in kind program or somebody identifies with the department that fulfill that role.

Transcript: Individual Interview
Control Number: 2013-09-(P9)
Research: Police Suicide: Acuity of Influence
By: Michael J. Alicea, MS, MSW

DEMOGRAPHICS
Gender: Male
Race and or Ethnicity: White
Age: 36-45
Current Marital Status: Married
Education - Highest Degree Held: JD
Employment: Coral Gables Police Department, State of Florida
Type of Law Enforcement Agency: Municipal Agency
Title: Police Lieutenant
Length of Service: 15 years or more

I: *What type(s) of difficult situations have you or another police officer have you come across in your law enforcement career that would lead you to consider suicide as a choice?*
P9: My professional career in law enforcement? Never, never considered.

I: *In retrospect to your experience with your present law enforcement organization, what type of in-service educational program did you undertake concerning the topic of suicide?*
P9: None. Nothing.

I: *Thinking back on the training you received with your present agency, what could have been done to improve and enhance the efficacy of the suicide education (if any)?*
P9: Well, they should have, I think they should have a class, at least once a year, to talk about the issue, they never talk about it, and, maybe they should have, or be visible and explain how people who have a problem and how easy it is to get therapy. Like I said, talk about it.

I: *Considering your experience with the agency you are employed with, in what ways does your police organization demonstrate concern about your welfare and on the issue of suicide?*
P9: None at all. None at all.

I: *What efforts do your peers do to diminish the strains that depression often exert on fellow officers that may consider suicide as an option?*

P9: None at all either. That's something I've not seen. I've been in law enforcement for 23 years and that's something that the only time its seen is when something happens. When nothing happens, they don't talk about it. Nobody talks about it.

I: *How do you view the police culture encumbering an officer's from ability to look for help on the subject of suicide?*

P9: Well, I can't really talk too much about that, because I don't know what happens in closed rooms when they talk about different types of training, and different types of things they can do for the officer, I don't know what they talk about. So, I really can't say. All I know is that I've never seen anything put out or any type of training or anytime anything to talk about it, discussions about it, I've never seen any effort at all by the police department to do anything about it. With fellow officers, once again, that's not talked about. It's just like nobody wears a vest until somebody gets shot. All of a sudden somebody gets shot, and everyone wears a vest for two months, and after that it goes away and nobody is wearing a vest again. And that's the same rule with that. Somebody commits suicide, and all of a sudden everybody talks about it, and after a while it goes away, and nobody talks about it anymore.

I: *In retrospect to your experiences with your present law enforcement organization, what types of training programs have you had that would have addressed the issue of suicidal thoughts?*

P9: None.

I: *How do police supervisors and command staff speak to the issue of police officer suicide in your law enforcement organization?*

P9: They don't. They never say one word about it. They don't.

I: *How can police supervisors and command staff ward off the risk of suicide as an option for your fellow officers?*

P9: Well, I think the supervisors could be more in tune to their subordinates, to see what's going on in their lives. They don't have to get personal, but if they see somebody change a little bit they should get more involved and talk to the person about their problem, and then talk to them about getting help, but in this department, it is not that way. The supervisor cares about you being on time, that you don't cause any problems, answer your radio, and that you don't have to call them. Write a report or something, that's all they care about, they don't care about how you're doing.

Transcript: Individual Interview
Control Number: 2013-10-(P10)
Research: Police Suicide: Acuity of Influence
By: Michael J. Alicea, MS, MSW

DEMOGRAPHICS
Gender: Male
Race and or Ethnicity: African American
Age: 46-55
Current Marital Status: Married
Education - Highest Degree Held: High School
Employment: Coral Gables Police Department, State of Florida
Type of Law Enforcement Agency: Municipal Agency
Title: Police Officer
Length of Service: 25 years or more

I: *What type(s) of difficult situations have you or another police officer have you come across in your law enforcement career that would lead you to consider suicide as a choice?*
P10: Nothing. I would never do that.

I: *In retrospect to your experience with your present law enforcement organization, what type of in-service educational program did you undertake concerning the topic of suicide?*
P10: None that I know of.

I: *Thinking back on the training you received with your present agency, what could have been done to improve and enhance the efficacy of the suicide education (if any)?*
P10: I guess it would improve if it actually existed. It doesn't. We haven't had any training.

I: *Considering your experience with the agency you are employed with, in what ways does your police organization demonstrate concern about your welfare and on the issue of suicide?*
P10: I've never heard anything about it.

I: *What efforts do your peers do to diminish the strains that depression often exert on fellow officers that may consider suicide as an option?*
P10: Is that personal experience or...? Read it again. I don't think I've ever experienced that. I've never had an issue or seen that.

I: *How do you view the police culture encumbering an officer's from ability to look for help on the subject of suicide?*
P10: Again, without the experience or knowledge about such a situation where I have been involved in, it's almost like it's not applicable.

I: *In retrospect to your experiences with your present law enforcement organization, what types of training programs have you had that would have addressed the issue of suicidal thoughts?*
P10: None. More dealing with the public than dealing with ourselves.

I: *How do police supervisors and command staff speak to the issue of police officer suicide in your law enforcement organization?*
P10: It hasn't happened. Never happened.

I: *How can police supervisors and command staff ward off the risk of suicide as an option for your fellow officers?*
P10: Offer a program, someone to speak to, Umm, I don't see it being an issue here, then again, at least, it would be a personal issue, talk to a close friend as opposed to..... I don't know anyone in the Charlie shift that's needing,(names a number of police officers on his shift who he can depend on for help), the people I work with I would probably notice something, I don't think I've had that experience, on a shift. Right of course, the administration can do a better job at making us aware of suicide by creating a program maybe having a training, even a roll call training, just something, you know, to let everyone know that something is available just in case they happen to feel that way (suicidal thoughts). A pamphlet, I think something like that needs to exists in our department. I don't think it would take a lot of money, I don't think it could be done in a half an hour, at least an introduction, maybe a book, a program or a video or something. At least letting people know that something exists that's there if you need it. Like our legal assistance, something like that, I guess.

Transcript: Individual Interview
Control Number: 2013-11-(P11)
Research: Police Suicide: Acuity of Influence
By: Michael J. Alicea, MS, MSW

DEMOGRAPHICS
Gender: Male
Race and or Ethnicity: Hispanic
Age: 46-55
Current Marital Status: Married
Education - Highest Degree Held: AA
Employment: Coral Gables Police Department, State of Florida
Type of Law Enforcement Agency: Municipal Agency
Title: Police Sergeant
Length of Service: 10 years or more

I: *What type(s) of difficult situations have you or another police officer have you come across in your law enforcement career that would lead you to consider suicide as a choice?*
P11: I haven't encountered anything that would lead me to consider suicide. I would imagine, and I'm sure people have said the same thing, because you are saying you could have, either did or could have, meaning what is possible that could happen should I consider suicide. You know, I would imagine, If I killed a kid, if I shot an innocent kid, you know, suicide, yeah, I don't think I ever consider suicide. Yeah, I don't think so.

I: *In retrospect to your experience with your present law enforcement organization, what type of in-service educational program did you undertake concerning the topic of suicide?*
P11: No, none.

I: *Thinking back on the training you received with your present agency, what could have been done to improve and enhance the efficacy of the suicide education (if any)?*
P11: Read that again. Provided.

I: *Considering your experience with the agency you are employed with, in what ways does your police organization demonstrate concern about your welfare and on the issue of suicide?*
P11: I mean they have the contact reports, they have the red flag that comes up, if you have a number of complaints, you know, you know if you got three, Umm, let's say you get three rudeness complaints, within three month period, then

you're supposed to sit down with that person (supervisor) and ask if everything is okay. Have the Employee Assistance Program (EAP), you know, there are programs in place to provide assistance. It's just a matter of that person coming forward, showing signs, you know, that they need it. I think there are things in place.

I: *What efforts do your peers do to diminish the strains that depression often exert on fellow officers that may consider suicide as an option?*
P11: I've never experienced that. You're saying what my coworkers have done for someone who wanted to attempt suicide, but I don't know anyone or anybody other than, (long pause), I really don't know anyone like that.

I: *How do you view the police culture encumbering an officer's from ability to look for help on the subject of suicide?*
P11: Read it again. Encumbering? Say it one more time. No, I don't know, you know our personalities, it's just a show of weakness, so, is that what you're getting at? You don't want to tell anybody that you're having problems.

I: *In retrospect to your experiences with your present law enforcement organization, what types of training programs have you had that would have addressed the issue of suicidal thoughts?*
P11: I'm trying to think if I'd had anything. May not be something that the City puts on, I attended something, no, no, no, and maybe they sent me to a class that I asked for. I'm not saying something that everybody took, and trying to think of some of my classes (long pause), yeah, maybe a command staff course, I took stress management class, IT may have mentioned depression or suicide that kind of thing, I don't recall if they told me much about suicide. I can't think of any.

I: *How do police supervisors and command staff speak to the issue of police officer suicide in your law enforcement organization?*
P11: I mean you know it's not something that people will talk about. So I, I don't know.

I: *How can police supervisors and command staff ward off the risk of suicide as an option for your fellow officers?*
P11: Provide training. Suicide prevention, suicide information, resources we have available, I mean resources like EAP, sure. Something they can add in the Academy. It was not in my Academy. Yes.

APPENDIX G: TRANSCRIPT: FOCUS GROUP INTERVIEWS

Transcript: Focus Group Interviews
Control Number: 2013-12-(P12)

DEMOGRAPHICS
Gender: Male
Race and or Ethnicity: White Hispanic
Age: 46-55
Current Marital Status: Married
Education - Highest Degree Held: BS
Employment: Coral Gables Police Department, State of Florida
Type of Law Enforcement Agency: Municipal Agency
Title: Police Officer
Length of Service: 25 years or more

Transcript: Focus Group Interviews
Control Number: 2013-13-(P13)

DEMOGRAPHICS
Gender: Male
Race and or Ethnicity: White
Age: 46-55
Current Marital Status: Married
Education - Highest Degree Held: AA
Employment: Coral Gables Police Department, State of Florida
Type of Law Enforcement Agency: Municipal Agency
Title: Police Officer
Length of Service: 25 years or more

Transcript: Focus Group Interviews
Control Number: 2013-14-(P14)

DEMOGRAPHICS
Gender: Male
Race and or Ethnicity: White
Age: 46-55
Current Marital Status: Married
Education - Highest Degree Held: MA
Employment: Coral Gables Police Department, State of Florida

Type of Law Enforcement Agency: Municipal Agency
Title: Police Officer
Length of Service: 25 years or more

Transcript: Focus Group Interviews
Control Number: 2013-15-(P15)

DEMOGRAPHICS
Gender: Male
Race and or Ethnicity: White
Age: 46-55
Current Marital Status: Married
Education - Highest Degree Held: BA
Employment: Coral Gables Police Department, State of Florida
Type of Law Enforcement Agency: Municipal Agency
Title: Police Sergeant - Retired
Length of Service: 25 years or more

I: *What type(s) of difficult situations have you or another police officer have you come across in your law enforcement career that would lead you to consider suicide as a choice?*

P12: I would say in my career, none. It's been more personal.

P13: Twenty-six years, I've done a lot. There's a lot of stress involved here. Outside, it affects a great deal. We've talked about this before. We go to work and there is nothing but stress. You go to work with more stress. There was a point there, when I was on day shift, the one that stuck out, that there were two Latin women who made a left turn on New Year's Eve and they got T-boned by a DUI. Of course, nobody knew, the whole family was at the house celebrating New Year's. I had to go and knock on their door, the door opens, and there's is this whole family there, all of a sudden they started screaming and crying the husband walked up to me, he just looked at me, I didn't say nothing. They're dead aren't they? I didn't say anything. How the fuck do you answer that? You see all this stress and shit, and everything else, you see a lot of things, you respond to it, you become cold, cynical, all that shit, but does it mean anything to you suicide? I mean I've been stressed out, depressed, I've seen a therapist, has it gotten to that point, no. Can I see it getting to that point, maybe not for me, based on what we do, maybe not for me, but I can see that happening. Based on what we do, maybe we don't expect it because it's the Gables, and not much could happen here, like Miami, they work in a combat zone like in Liberty City (high crime area in Miami), I can see them "spazing out." You got financial issues, you're going to lose your house, you know your kids and wife are affected, going at it, do I see it happening, yes. Knock on wood, I've never contemplated it.

P12: I think our environment, might have a lot to do with that. Like he just elaborated on, we're not in the shit hole, like Miami, or the County. We don't see that death and gore that they see daily. When I was going through my low times, fortunate for me we did not have that many stressful situations. Could I see it, yeah? If I was working for Miami and in Liberty City, yeah. The County or Brownsville or something. We don't have that environment. I'll be really honest, I'm not religious. I don't really have one view on suicide. I was born Methodist.

P14: I think that because there are Catholics here (referring to the police officers in the focus group), that suicide is not always a viable option. I've been surrounded by suicide my whole life. My football practice coach, maybe here, suicide is the common denominator here. Nevertheless....

P13: What were you looking at me for, I wasn't going to say anything.

P14: The doctor that delivered you committed suicide (laugh).

P13: Can you lean back a little bit.

P14: My college girlfriend, who I was head over heels in love with, her brother committed suicide.

P12: Hey, can I give you my guns tonight? (laugh)

P14: It never got to that level for me at any point; and Umm, through the good and the bad at work. It never got to that level. There have been some depression and anger, there's been all those feelings, that's the tipping point, it just never got to that point. It doesn't mean that it won't ever, I'm not worried about you guys, I'm worried about you guys getting in your 60s and 70s and then pulling the pin because, you know, because....

P13: I don't want to say there is fear or concern, there's a, fear, but when you start getting older, if you can't do things that you used to do when you were younger, you can't take care of yourself, you know Umm, there's a question of being a burden, you know, and suicide, going quietly into that good night. Umm, there was this guy who was moving with his daughter, and all that shit, she was terminal and fucked up, and the night before, they all went out to dinner, they went home, they all said good night to each other, and that night she shot herself. When I walked into the house, to check on her well-being, I walked into the house, the AC was set at freezing, everyplace in the house were postem notes, this is for(directions on who gets what and when), she was on a La-Z-Boy, she put a towel over her head, she shot herself. She had a letter, I remember looking at it, it's fucked up. Her daughter was outside the room, I would not let her come in, and I thought about that. Is there a remote possibility, absolutely (thoughts about suicide)? I'm not going to sit there, what he (P12) said, that environment that you're in, I think it's cold, despite the fact that we may be a little bit more educated, we can fall into that, resorting to that. I think that we realize that there are more outs. Again, if you kill yourself, will your wife be home, kids, really... I just think...

P14: I think for me, Umm, I really don't define myself in this job. I've done a good job, the best! I was productive. I was really committed to what I was doing.

I'm still committed to what I'm doing, I never really defined myself by this job, I think that part, that identity outside of work, how we see ourselves, those are the guys that can handle it. The guys who can't let go of this job....

P13: Can't separate...

P14: So intertwined in this job, and I worry about these guys, and people who start out being explorers, wanting to become cops, they become cops forever, and in some of our cases, stuff that happened years ago, nonetheless...

P13: There is an officer, he was a cop 24/7, he was in the uniform all the time, his kids are away at college, there's is a domestic situation at his home, they become separated in time (husband and wife), he doesn't have a life outside of this. The last time I talked to him, he was separated, living in an efficiency, dude, you've got nobody to blame but yourself. You know, like, the stressors get you, you mention (P12) that officer who had killed himself because of a pending divorce, you throw in a "fuckin" medical problem and shit, add financial problems, it's, how well your put together.

P14: I think the four of us, we've slipped in under the wire, we've been bruised up and banged up, but still able to get to the DROP (retirement program), into the pension, whereas a lot of guys ten to fifteen years behind, are fucked (referring to pension plan drawback). They're in a serious financial burden, and other issues, beyond their realm of handling.

P13: It's society too, the generation, this generation, you get the old school guys, for us, the old school guys are us.

P12: But I think also, again, times have changed. Back in the old timers, those that taught us, they would say you're going to get help for what, you can help yourself? Nowadays, getting help is not so bad.

P14: My opinion goes two ways, like he said (P12), whether you're crazy, went to Korea, went to Vietnam, now the pendulum has swung this way, swinging the other way...

P13: There's that the new generation, people are coming out, they're not even making the effort, to be responsible, accountability for your actions and everything else. It's a quick fix, they're not even making the effort as before (when they were rookies), it's like, but Humm...(stops suddenly).

I: *In retrospect to your experience with your present law enforcement organization, what type of in-service educational program did you undertake concerning the topic of suicide?*

P12: None

P13: None, I think back about when McEvoy died, a Major of Uniform Patrol said, a quote that he was a loner.

P14: I saw McEvoy, two days before, a civilian tried to walk up to the door of the rear of the station, and he says: (McEvoy yells out) "Hey, we're not opened yet." The person looks back, wrong building. That van (automobile where police officer committed suicide) was littered with cigarette wrappers, coke cans and ashes everywhere. I mean you can tell that he was smoking and he said: "This place doesn't care about the "family man." I said to myself, "something's wrong with this guy." He was having a hard time with child care, and I said, why not put him in an administrative job for the summer, he can still do his 59's (Off-Duty Jobs) with weekends off, and be able to transition and deal with his child care problem.....it will at least get him through the summer. I'm telling you again, I think back, he could have been gunning for somebody in particular....I think he just lost his nerve.

P12: We don't know that.

P14: There was a mechanism to prevent this. Like my wife said, and I agree with her, when you are not feeling well, when someone is in a room for a long time, with someone who screams and hollers' all the time, stuck in a room all the time, it wears on them.

P12: Unintelligible...

P14: He was forced to take days off, he had seniority, he had to burn his hours to have weekends off, and then he went into the child care issue. It's ridiculous, because we're a self-insured City, you can put anyone you want in that car, it doesn't make a difference. You think that anyone in CID(Criminal Investigations Division) or anywhere else doesn't take their kids to school before going to work...come on.

P13: A Sergeant from CID had a unmarked car and took his kids to school, I "fuckin" did it. How many years do you think I did that?

P14: Eight years...I got news for you, you expect me to take action out there, so I already have my radio, I put my kids in my car, you want me to take action, give me the tools to do it.

P15: Preventive training program....when did that come out? (Laughing) When did that come out? (Laughing)

P13: I missed that. (Laughing)

P15: That must have come out when I retired.

I: *Thinking back on the training you received with your present agency, what could have been done to improve and enhance the efficacy of the suicide education (if any)?*

P12: Aside from working with certain people...

P13: That goes to the human diversity shit, touchy, feeling, everything else and all of this shit, Crisis Intervention Training for Baker Act's, nobody touched that, suicide prevention. Stress relations for officers and shit. What's there, oh yeah, stress kills.

P12: We don't have no transition courses, you retired, ok, you did a great job. I mean...

P15: We don't even get that (Laughing).

P12: Somebody like (referring to an Officer in the Focus Group), I mean, some of us who got out, it's not going to be too difficult, but the other people that have no "outs" have no other life, hey, now you're on your own.

P14: You know, I worked VIN (Vice and Narcotics), traveled to Montreal, New York, Houston, had credit cards, cars, all of a sudden they go "boom" now it's all taken away from you. But, when there was no position, and the overtime is cut on the fourth floor, Skinner (The Chief of Police) wants to bring in counselors to help people adjust to the losses, but they don't do anything for McEvoy. Right now, being a year and three quarters from the DROP, they should be having a dual prong approach to your transition out.

P13: Everybody should be on a transitional program.

P14: We should be having a program that helps this guy take a position, but they don't. There should be a kind of a program where you hold the door and while he (officer who is in need of help) is going out the door (retirement).

I: *Considering your experience with the agency you are employed with, in what ways does your police organization demonstrate concern about your welfare and on the issue of suicide?*

P13: Read that question again.

P13: Stop right there, they don't'. Suicide is part of everything that you have to do. As for our agency, you're looked as if you're disposable, you're in the DROP, and they don't care.

P15: The old timers didn't have this issue, at least if you had some issues; they worked with you, around your schedule, or different things. The new regimen, the new "puck kids" coming up, they don't, they don't have no camaraderie, and they don't care about anybody.

P12: Last year was the first time our department contributed to our EAP. The first time ever and how long did it take you to ask them, our department to do that (Reference Retirement Seminar offered)? Last year was the first time that our own psychologist came to our police department, to introduce themselves to say what this is, what the program is, this is what we can do, here's my phone number, here's my card.

P14: Let me ask you a question, you, you, and you, who really believes that EAP is really confidential? (Laughter among all the officers in the focus group).

P15: Oh no, I don't believe that it is.

P14: I don't think it's totally confidential. I think the Chief, the Major and HR gets (interrupted)…

P12: It depends, let me finish…You say a certain "buzz" word",…let me finish, I don't mind telling everybody here, I've been to our guy twice over my career. Both for my son. If it was a work related issue, or something, no, I don't think its confidential at all, but me going to him, Hey, (referring to the psychologist he spoke to), this is what's going on, yes, it's confidential. He (Commander) has the sole right to pick up the phone, to call the City Manager or Human Resource to say, take him off the road. It's his obligation.

P14: You say the wrong thing, therefore, even the sweetest guy that you may be, you may be pulling back with what truly is going to help you with the issues because you know that the consequences are going to transcend beyond your…(Interrupted)

P13: If you want to get help, you're going to have to tap dance around it, we're not stupid here. You know you go in and say that some days you just want to go "postal" (a termed often coined and referred to Postal Workers losing control) on the third floor (where the Chief of Police Office is at)…(Laughter among all the officers in the focus group).

P13: Yeah, ok, are you just playing or are you serious about that? (Laughter among all the officers in the focus group)

P13: It's not even like you go down the roster, if he says that, he's just "fuckin" around, but if he says that, you take that serious, if anybody says that, you take that serious, but if anybody says that,…(interrupted).

P15: I've made more of an effort to think and understand what is happening out there….

P14: My first shooting, I was walking through the basement, a Sergeant who was parking, came up to me, saw me walking, made a beeline turn, he said, "I want to ask you about what happened here." I said, "ok," well Sergeant, I mean Humm, what do you think about what happened? You know, I come from law enforcement, I come from smart people, well, an exact quote: "I feel like I was working within the scope and ability of my training," and he goes, "you know, you almost killed somebody?" Yeah, and he said: "How do you feel about that?" I said: "I was working with the skills of my employment." He said: "Well, maybe we should schedule an appointment to see the psychologist," and I said: "You know what; you can do that because you're the Sergeant." I said: "I've got a "news flash" for you; I've got friends that I drink iced tea and have a beer with that I have more going on with them that than some guy that has a diploma on the wall. You want me to go see him, I'll go see him, I have a support network outside of this job that supports me, and takes care of me very well. He then said: "Whenever you want to have a beer with me, you let me know." (Laughter among all the officers in the focus group)

P13: You have to have, you have to have a certain trust, comfort and rapport, you have to have a certain, we all have this in common, do you have that with the psychologist, (unintelligible)…that's not going to happen. We used to have a "Choir Practice," with people you know, Choir Practice was great, because, everybody would "BS," you'd vent, basically it would be a venting session, you'd get it out of your system.

P12: I think I only met him (psychologist)once, when I did my psychological (pre-screening for employment), he just made me feel so uncomfortable talking, I don't know what it was, now this psychologist (new psychologist via EAP) was just the opposite, he took over for the other psychologist, and he was just…interrupted.

P14: If you brought me in, he'd give you the MMPI (Minnesota Multiphasic Personality Inventory (MMPI), so I sat down, and I looked at his diploma on the wall, and I said, oh, you went to (referring to the university where the psychologist obtained his degree in psychology), and he (psychologist) said, "your familiar with it?" Yes, I played soccer against them, I always thought that it was a "party school." I always thought that it stood for you should set your hand stamped instead of a diploma"), and he got "fuckin" nasty, he tried to not get me hired because I said that.

P13: If your gonna, your gonna have a program, something in place, he's (psychologist) is just treating people.

P14: Let's look at something else, why is our Internal Affairs in our building? Every police department's Internal Affairs should be off-site.

P12: Stop it, your making sense, you can't do that, stop it!

P13: What he said is a joke, but it's the absolute truth. If it makes sense, they overlook it. You know, and they know it, but they do it anyway. We're back to the previous question, and you file grievances, and for what? Too bad, change it….it doesn't get better, God forbid if some of these people come forward with their problems, do you think that these young guys can do this? You think that they can do this? Anything can happen.

P14: Plus, you have people who are tragically dysfunctional, flawed, beyond belief, Lieutenants, Majors, tragically flawed. I mean that, I mean, I'll say this, we're all old guys, friends, we're all valuable friends, yes, I'm (referring to his present assignment), but if you think that all I do you are wrong. I'm surrounded by intelligence, you're out of your mind, and, the stuff that is coming across my desk, across my PC, related to this building, you'd be amazed. Some of these people should never have been hired, and were recommended that they not be hired, and now are your Lieutenants, your Majors…

P13: You don't think that "frost my balls"…(interrupted)

P14: I've got to see that (Laughter).

P13: A little frosting….

P12: That's a damn image to see(Laughter).

P13: I see people here, and I look back at all the people that I have trained with, look at some of these people that I'm… how, why, these are the same people who, this is what's… they're not even meaningless…..it's like…(interrupted).

P15: That "shit" has gotten out of control…right now.

P13: Back to the other question, common sense issues here….

P14: They're shock by their own truth…

P13: Exactly right, we joke about it, but really, we're at combat arms, how many "friendly fire" (referring to accidental shootings) "fuckin" accidents happened here? No really, you got to say it, it's like from the movie the "Dirty Dozen" Charles Bronson says, this guy did this, this and this, and I shot him while we were going over the hill, all these soldiers were going over the hill and getting killed because of him. The Major says, the only mistake you did was letting someone see you when you shot him. You know, I mean, yeah, I mean.....there are people here that you want to take out and beat the shit out of them. You want to tell them, dude, you're "fuckin" hurting everybody, physically, emotionally, psychological-ly, department wide, you're killing us. And, and, your "fuckin" DUI, "fuckin" around on your wife, doing donuts with an unmarked police car on a golf course, you get stopped by another agency, and driven home, and then you got the balls to come to "fuckin" roll call and talk to us about ethics and camaraderie. I'm mean, I'm ready for lightening to strike, it's like, "karma is a bitch," unfortunately, for-tunately, I won't be here long enough to see any of that stuff come to fruition.

P15: I know that case, the problem is that the dude got arrested, and nothing ever happens (laughter)....you bastards.

P12: You know, he just said something that me and (referring to P13) talk about all the time, but, nothing, ever, ever happens to these people.

P15: That's because they're in that click with the regime.

P12: It's all "poppy cup," it's all part of they do stuff that nothing ever happens to them.

P14: To "dove tail" what (referring to P12) just said, it doesn't mean that they're just bad people, (refers to specific command staff by name), and a few others, and they all came up with, they all have weekends and holidays off, and they make the decisions for the greater amount of officers. They'll say to you, hey you that has twenty-six years, you go to back to the road.

P13: Some young officer will complain that they have been here fifteen years, complaining that they can't get weekends. "What the fuck!"

P12: I'm going to echo what these guys are saying, but we're willing to do what's best for the department, these guys were given weekend from the get go. Now, you try to take it away, are you kidding me, I was promised the weekends. No-body promised you anything.

P13: But in the end, they're not paying attention to the needs of the people that made this department.

P14: We had an applicant last month, oral interview, the Major said: "What will you bring to our department?" The applicant said: "What are you going to do for me?" The Major just looked up, and walked out. The same applicant was pro-cessed at Metro-Dade (Reference the County Sherriff's Department), a close friend to the County Manager and the County Mayor, they don't know what to do with him, and he's already in the academy. This is the mindset that's coming out here. This, this mentality.....the problems is, what should be said, I don't care who your dad knows, get the "fuck" out of here.

P15: There should be no favoritism; he's got to stay in one zone, like me, like everyone else, if you're new, north, old south.

P13: The lack of leadership here, and everything.

P15: The nine, the ten and days off, and now they're going back to eight (referring to hours in a shift), they're not taking into consideration the hardships that this causes.

P14: There is a reversal of the gentrifrication. The old guys, twenty-six years and on, are handling the calls for service, the young guys are doing nothing. You've severed the lifeblood of the agency, he going to walk out (pointing and referring to each officer in the focus group), he's going to walk out, now what are you going to do?

P15: It's a shame to what's happened to this place. They question everything, its ok to question everything, the way that they question things today, Can you imagine going to (referring to a veteran old retired Sergeant) and saying that…(laughter).

P12: You see there is a little difference here; I would never question anything you tell me as a supervisor (referring to the retired supervisor in the focus group), because I respect you. Some of these young supervisors, who you know don't do the right thing…

P15: That's right, sometimes I go to some of the "old timers" and they say, what do we got here, you know, we talk about it, now we have these new supervisors who don't have a "fuckin" clue what to do, and they say: "This is what we're going to do." Are you kidding me you know.

P14: We had a training exercise, where a chlorine truck had a spill, and the officer went to a new Sergeant to look for answers in handling this situation , the Sergeant was buried in the SOP (Standard Operating Procedures), he was clueless. I lean over to him and I suggest a number of things that he may want to consider. He's a new supervisor and he doesn't know what to do because he has no experience on the road.

I: *What efforts do your peers do to diminish the strains that depression often exert on fellow officers that may consider suicide as an option?*

P12: I'll be honest…I,I..I work with a veteran squad in the last three, four, five years, and we get together on a daily basis, whether we go down to Matheson Hammocks for ten or fifteen minutes, or even twenty minutes, all of us, smoking cigars, whatever, but that's what we do. I mean, that officer (referring once again to an officer in the group) has been there a lot for me. I've been there a lot for another officer (referring to another officer in the group), that officer (referring to an officer not in the group), believe it or not, he's not a bad guy, if you really get to know him. We all got to know them, because we would all go to Matheson Hammocks for five or ten minutes, twenty minutes a day, and we would "freakin" debrief, and distress, whatever.

P13: To expand on that, we talk about everything. Peers, we are the peers. Today, nobody has peers that "sucks." We talk about everything that's happening in individually. Suicide, it has to come up because of situations, like I said, situations generally speaking, what's happening if someone was right there, it would be us talking about it. And I'll tell you "flat out," if I see someone who has the tendency, down that path, I'm going to intervene. Somehow, I'm going to do something about it.

P14: To the best of our abilities, we all try...

P15: I can't tell you how many times I helped that bastard (referring to officer that committed suicide).

P13: That comes down to just us. How much power do we have to do something? You know, we want to help somebody, if it comes to that point, I'll pitch a fit.

P15: At the very heart of it, I had a good friend of mine who blew his brains out, and nobody realized it. You know, there were signs there. You don't look at your own people and say man, that guy is not doing well.

P13: But you see, there's nothing in place, nobody knows how to get to that person, nobody knows how to initiate it.

P15: Remember, Cops are a different breed than the general public, because, we're more guarded than the general public. We can walk down the street, and you can see that this person is off his rocker, but Cops are more guarded, we really have to be more trained in the law enforcement aspects. I remember Peppy (referring to an officer who committed suicide), the only thing that they knew about Peppy, was that at one point he was depressed, he really was kind of hallucinating, he was an alcoholic, going through rehab. Ok, and there was all kinds of rumors flying that because he was involved in Task Force, that he went to the other side, that he was involved in stuff. When I pulled his autopsy report, which "pissed off" a lot of people off, I wanted to know if he was on drugs. What happens, ahhhh, he wasn't on alcohol, for a guy who was an alcoholic, I used to drink with him all the time. Ahhh, he was straight, his blood alcohol was straight, nothing in it, ahhh, drugs came back as nothing, and they "fucked up," because it was, the doctor that he was seeing on the side, the doctor said take him off the road and administration kept bugging him when you coming back, when you coming back, and they never did anything. What happened was, he was so into depression, the doctor gave him a sample drug at the office that made him hallucinate. To the point where he went to church and blew his brains out, on-duty and at the...no, no, he was trying to get out, back to the road, he wanted to get out. Other issues were, they found out where he lived and they (drug lords) put a knife through his cat and stuck it on the front door to his house. You know, they killed his cat, and stuck it on his front door, his wife discovered it, he said afterward: "That's it, we're moving, I want to give up this end of it (undercover work), go back to patrol." But they (administration) wouldn't let him. They kept hounding him, to go back, it stressed him out, the stress finally got him, and nobody realized it until it happened, oh yeah, they didn't do anything.

P13: Long story short, their (administration) ignoring it, they're not doing anything about it. They wait for the crash; look at McEvoy, what was done? Nothing!

P15: Nothing.

P13: Nothing has been done. You know, it's like, you keep asking, you keep looking, to all of these questions, everything, it's all symptomatic, the problem is, they use you up. You know, it's not just, they don't' do the minimum of what they have to do. Yeah....that's what, that's what...that's what it all comes down to. For being such an accredited agency, oh my God, this and that, its bullshit!

P14: McEvoy, had he been smart, he would have gotten into the patrol car, at three o'clock in the afternoon, at the intersection of Lejeune and U.S. 1 (the busiest intersection during rush hour traffic in the City of Coral Gables), and start singing Opera, ok, and when the news helicopter films us forcibly extracting him out of his patrol car he would have gotten full disability and some, and would have been taken care of.

I: *How do you view the police culture encumbering an officer's from ability to look for help on the subject of suicide?*

P14: If your number one on the lieutenant's list and you reveal to the department that you have a problem, you're not going to get promoted.

P12: I think that it's a little bit better today, than it was back then, again when we first started, cause, back then, and even now, we're more equip to handle somebody else's problem, compared to ours. Because we're taught to handle everybody else's problem, we're not taught to handle our own, and we don't seek help; it can get to you a little bit.

P13: You become invisible.

P14: Then you become vulnerable.

P12: That all depends who you are?

P13: Well, that's what I'm saying, ok, you see, that's it, that's the reaction, that happens, unless, case in point, you're in a unmark car, making donuts, DUI, you know what, they'll give it to you, or a bottle of Jack Daniels...

P14: Or hugging a bottle of Jack Daniels at a seminar that I attended with this person.

P12: A perfect example is, if it was (referring to an officer in the group) or myself, we've probably be taken off the road or something. We have a guy in patrol, I'm not going to mention his name, that there's no question, has PTSD, a Sergeant is totally aware of it, he's supposedly seeking help, but he's still on the road today.

P13: You know, there's been some issues where you want to say that a 34 (signal that denotes a domestic and or quarrel that is ensuing), in roll-call, but it's getting to the point that everybody follows the leader. It's very emotional, it's very dangerous, because, we're all armed, you know, a fist fight is one thing, your that emotional, your that "fucked up," whatever, how do act when your.... unintelligible.

P12: This guy just recently got into a major 34 with a supervisor, and it was swept underneath the carpet because the Major told everybody to do it. I mean, it's well-known, well it's not well known, but the supervisor is aware of it, and when it was brought to my attention, I looked at this certain supervisor, I said, what are you going to do about it? Because if you don't do something about it, then I might. He said I'll take care of it; I'll take care of it. Well, I don't know if it's being taken care of.

I: *In retrospect to your experiences with your present law enforcement organization, what types of training programs have you had that would have addressed the issue of suicidal thoughts?*
P12: None.
P13: None
P14: None
P15: None.
P13: Let me go back to that, for us in particular......look at McEvoy, lost in the process.

I: *How do police supervisors and command staff speak to the issue of police officer suicide in your law enforcement organization?*
P12: None.
P13: None, we don't. Nobody even talks about it. With McEvoy, nobody mentions his name. When was the last time the department ever mentioned his name?
P14: I don't even know if he warrants a plaque in the front lobby, but something should have been said or done.
P13: People on up there (names of fallen officers on wall) have died on duty, one who died while jogging on-duty; it wasn't in the line of duty, but on-duty. For the grace of God, that could be me, that could be you, and this, it has been twenty-six years, half my life, it's a shame that there's nothing in place.

I: *How can police supervisors and command staff ward off the risk of suicide as an option for your fellow officers?*
P14: Let me ask you this, we have these guys, Chaplains in names only, but when you go to a meeting, not that those guys are bad guys, but some of these guys are so impervious, using the word God, they pontificate....interrupted.
P13: Let me break a rule hear, you got (identifies a lieutenant by name) quoting scripture, who something, ok, I'll break another rule; I'll call it the "Spencer Rule" (denotes an unofficial position of wanting to not see an officer work in the department, and rather than discharging them, the City will pay the officer to stay home , collect a pay check, work off-duty, until they reach retirement eligibility).

You want to do something, put something in place. All this diversity training, all this "bullshit," you know what, a little less "Sir" could you please stop acting that way, Put the information out there, there's nothing.

P12: But you got to make our supervisors aware of what's going on.

P14: We put more effort into Robert Brightman (a chronic homeless person).(Laughter among all the officers in the focus group)than we did for McEvoy.

P12: You just said something, that guy at Douglas and Miracle Mile(referring to the chronic homeless person), they want us to write reports, make detailed notes, enter in our CAD (Computer Aided Dispatch), about this guy and what we want from this guy.

P13: They are not going to do anything, their documenting, we put him in the back of a car and take him somewhere, no, again, nothing. It's just "smoke and mirrors." Not even.

P12: I go back again to the environment we're in, but I'm going to tell you right now, when we first started here, until about five or six, seven years ago, every employee of our City was glad to come to work; and had positive attitude. From our garbage man, to our secretaries, right now, nobody can stand coming to work, because of this City Manager, when he's done, ahhh, and everything.

P13: It's not just the City, it's across the board. There's a running joke, look how many watch order (A specific area patrolled by a police officer during the regular course of a shift) there are, there's none at the City Manager's house, there's not a Cop standing outside his door. The other running joke, 225 and 168, there's not too many people who understand that joke here and that we even joke about that. When we make a joke, there's something behind the joke, and its frustration coming out of this and that, and again it comes back to they're not addressing any of this.

P12: What's going to happen October 1, when the general employees have to pay 27%, what's going to happen to them?

P15: One of them is going to commit suicide, or take him out (referring to the City Manager) or somebody else out.

P12: Seriously, and I agree with officer (referring to P13), it's not just our City Manager, the last true leader that we had at our department was, think about it, think about it, Chief Skalaski (Circa 1980's) maybe. Nobody knows what are then Chiefs that followed would have done, take him out of the equation, really. For us in this room, how about Chief Skalaski?

P14: How many Chiefs have we had? We've had about ten, and who really has been a true leader to us?

P12: A certain Major calls the Chief Skalaski about one of us not writing a report, he (Chief) agrees with this officer well, he shouldn't have written a report, goodbye.

P14: Yet, there was a certain faction, that wanted to get him out, and they brought in these moles, after he died. We have been rudderless, as he said earlier, self-autonomous, no pilot of the ship, we run our own show.

P12: That's a compliment to all of us here because we're running the ship.

P14: We'll actually, we keep the ship from hitting the rocks.

P12: We got a Major now, who wants us to bid without knowing where our supervisors are going. Well, they have never, ever done that.

P13: You not addressing the issue, we're not putting anything in place that there should be, and really, when you look at it, how hard would it be to put something in place?

End

4B www.herald.com SATURDAY, OCTOBER 23, 1999 F

Coral Gables police officer dies in apparent suicide near station

BY ARNOLD MARKOWITZ
AND ELAINE DE VALLE
amarkowitz@herald.com

Coral Gables Police Officer Thomas McEvoy apparently killed himself Friday morning in a city parking garage behind police headquarters, Miami-Dade Police said.

His body was discovered at 11:45 a.m. in the front seat of his Chevrolet van by another officer walking past it in a section where police vehicles are parked. The engine was running.

There was no suicide note in the van, and McEvoy's reason for killing himself was not immediately known. He was 47.

Deputy Chief Ana Baixauli said McEvoy had personal problems: "He was raising his kids by himself, and I don't think he had a whole lot of help, even though we all tried to help him."

McEvoy had been divorced twice, the last time in 1989, and had custody of his children. Baixauli said he did not know how many there were.

Miami-Dade County Police spokeswoman Nelda Fonticella said McEvoy was off duty. He apparently drove to the city garage specifically to die there.

Police did not describe the weapon he used, except to say it was not his police gun.

McEvoy lived in South Miami Heights. He had been a Coral Gables officer for about 15 years.

"He was a nice guy, but he was kind of a loner," the deputy chief said. "He was just to himself a lot. He showed up for work and did his job, but he wasn't one of those real popular guys. He had a lot of personal problems that obviously led to this tragic conclusion."

ACTIVIST ASKS CHIEF TO INVESTIGATE APPARENT SUICIDE OF VETERAN OFFICER

Miami Herald, The (FL) - Sunday, October 31, 1999
Author: BY CHARLES SAVAGE, csavage@herald.com

A prominent Coral Gables resident asked Police Chief Jim Skinner on Thursday for an independent investigation into last week's apparent suicide of a 17-year veteran officer.

The call for an investigation by retired activist Roxcy Bolton followed a week in which it has come to light that Officer Thomas McEvoy tried to commit suicide a year ago and in which rumors have circulated among city employees that he may have been involved in a federal investigation.

McEvoy 's body was found in the front seat of his Chevrolet van Oct. 22 in a city parking garage behind police headquarters. A medical examiner ruled the cause of death as a self-inflicted gunshot to the head. No suicide note was found.

Skinner said he investigated after Bolton brought the rumors to his attention. So far, he said Friday, he has found no evidence to support the widespread rumors that McEvoy may have been recently subpoenaed as a witness in a federal investigation against fellow police officers.

"At this point in time, I don't think there is a need for such a panel," Skinner said. "He was a good, solid patrol officer, and was not involved in any major cases that had the potential to rise to a federal level."

Skinner said Paul Mallett, assistant agent in charge of the FBI's Miami office, told him that McEvoy 's name does not appear anywhere in FBI files as a witness or subject of an investigation. He said he had also called the U.S. attorney, but had not received an answer by late Friday.

A police logbook of all subpoenas received by officers - kept by Patrol Division secretary Myra Quintero - contains no mention of McEvoy 's name in the days leading up to the suicide .

At a Coral Gables Citizens' Crime Watch luncheon Friday, First Assistant U.S. Attorney Guy Lewis said he had no knowledge of an investigation involving McEvoy or the Coral Gables Police Deparment.

Lewis delivered a keynote address discussing the fight against public corruption in South Florida in which he praised the Gables police as a "testament" to a "good, clean department."

But Bolton said that even if the more dramatic rumors about McEvoy proved false, she still saw the need for an inquiry.

"I asked the chief for an investigation by a panel of citizens and police," Bolton confirmed. "It is my understanding from reliable sources that he asked for medical retirement and he didn't get that because, it is alleged, that he had attempted suicide once before. And I believe when that happens with a police officer everything possible should be put in place to reinforce him."

Thomas McEvoy 's ex-wife Nancy McEvoy said that he had been troubled for some time and that he had slit his wrists a year ago, after which he was moved to a desk job and his department handgun was taken away.

"He was not a loner," she said. "He was very laid back, and with people who loved him and wanted to help him."

Benefits to McEvoy 's children, ages 12 and 13, have yet to be finalized. Don Nelson, finance director, said some retirement pension will go to them.

``The children will receive a benefit," Nelson said. ``The account is being calculated by an actuary, and it's not complete yet. But the children will receive a pension amount - both of them."

Herald writer Tere Figueres contributed to this report.

Memo: CORAL **GABLES**

Edition: Final
Section: Neighbors EA
Page: 2EA
Record Number: 9911050464
Copyright (c) 1999 The Miami Herald

CPSIA information can be obtained
at www.ICGtesting.com
Printed in the USA
BVOW10s0722200217

476269BV00008B/342/P